# ISLAMIC REPUBLIC OF IRAN & ERITREA: A GLIMPSE

# ISLAMIC REPUBLIC OF IRAN & ERITREA: A GLIMPSE

*Shankar Chatterjee*

SERIALS PUBLICATIONS
NEW DELHI (INDIA)

First Published - 2008

ISBN: 978-81-8387-120-4



*Published by*

**SERIALS PUBLICATIONS**
4830/24, Prahlad Street, Ansari Road
Darya Ganj, New Delhi-110002 (India)
Phone : 23245225 Fax : 91-11-23272135
E-mail: serials@satyam.net.in

# CONTENTS

# PREFACE

This book is the outcome of my visit to Islamic Republic Iran and the State of Eritrea. On invitation of the Ministry of Jihad for Agriculture, Government of Iran, I visited the country as Indian resource person in 2001. I stayed for about a month. On the other hand my assignment in Eritrea was for two years (February 2005 to January 2007) as Associate Professor in Economics. I was only person selected for the said post from entire India.

I enjoyed in both the countries, as people are soft-spoken, sober and hospitable. They have high regards for the Indians. Interestingly, in both the countries people like our Hindi movies. Many of them remember names of movies including actors and actresses. Even some of them recalled some Hindi dialogues from the movies.

In both the countries from the very first day I documented each and every incident of my visit. Based on my Iran visit I published an article in Indian journal and on Eritrea about 17 articles, I have published in newspaper of Eritrea (only English newspaper of Eritrea), Indian and USA journals. In this book the lone published article on Iran and few published articles on Eritrea are incorporated for the interest of readers.

I still cherish the sweet memories of my visit in both the countries, which I am sharing through this volume with the readers.

***Shankar Chatterjee***

# FOREWORD

Many travel far and wide in the world but very few observe men and manners, culture and tradition, landscape and history in minute details or have the urge to share their experiences with others. Dr. Shankar Chatterjee is one of those very few who has re-counted his experiences of his short stay in Iran and longer stay in Eritria with the richest of details. Because of his graphic description of both the places, the countries have come alive in the minds of the readers. The feeling is that of a virtually reality without physically visiting those places.

Dr. Shankar Chatterjee went to both the places on academic mission. He has shown the excitement and adventures-ness of a traveler while attending to his official duties. Since I have also visited Iran some time back I can identify my feelings of many of the aspects of Iran through his writings. The vast green parks of Iran, the great museums showing arte-facts and carpets of a 3,000 years old civilization, the celebrations and festivities, the snow-picks encircling the city of Tehran have become very vivid in his narration. His conscious, intelligent and observant visits can only bridge the gap of cultural prejudices.

Eritria is lesser known city in Africa and he has told the story of a lesser known people, who are mostly Muslims and Christians. As one reads through his document one feels that those countries match India in its great traditions of hospitality.

On the whole his documentation of both Iran and Eritrea is very informative and knowledge-based. In a very comprehensive way, he has studied the different facets of these two civilizations. It is a happy thing that he has decided to put all of his experiences in print so that others can also gain from his experiences.

I look forward to his traveling in many more countries in the World in future and bring out his experiences of those places. I wish him good luck in his endeavor.

**CHANDANA KHAN, I.A.S.**
Principal Secretary & Commissioner,
Govt. of Andhra Pradesh, Hyderabad

# ACKNOWLEDGEMENT

This is my second individual endeavour to publish the book at my own. Earlier I have published a book on self-help group based on my research study.

I would like to extend my sincere thanks to the Officials of Ministry of Jihad for Agriculture, Government of Iran and Ministry of Education, State of Eritrea for selecting me in their respective countries. I am thankful to the Ministry of Tourism, Eritrea for providing me necessary information. I express my deep gratitude to my uncle Shri Gurudas Chatterjee (former Civil Servant, Government of India) for greatly motivating me to publish the book.

My grateful thanks are due to Shri R.C. Choudhary, IAS, Ex-Director General of National Institute of Rural Development (NIRD), Hyderabad, then Deputy Director General, Shri Mathew C. Kunnumkal, IAS, Registrar, Mrs. Anita Karwal, IAS, and Director, Financial Management and Financial Adviser Mrs.V.Vedakumari, IA&AS, for permitting me to visit Iran.

I am greatly indebted vis-à-vis extend my grateful thanks to Shri Lalit Mathur, IAS, Former Director General of NIRD, then Deputy Director General, Shri Chinmay Basu, IAS, and Registrar, Shri G.V. Venugopala Sarma, IAS, NIRD for allowing me to join in Eritrea.

I express my grateful thanks to Shri V.S. Sampath, IAS, present Director General of NIRD, Shri Bhanwar Lal, I.A.S. Deputy Director General and Shri Sriram

Taranikanti Registrar and Director Financial Management and Financial Adviser for their encouragement in completing the volume.

I express my sincere thanks to Dr. S. Rajakutty, Professor and Director and Dr. (Mrs) Jaya Lakshmi (my Didi) of NIRD for inspiring me in publishing the volume. My grateful thanks are due to Shri D.V. Madhusudan Rao, Head-Department of Management, and Asmara Commercial College, Eritrea for his co-operation during the course of writing the book. He is working last 9 years in this country. I am thankful to Mr. Tewolde Tesfamariam, Head-Department of English, EIT and Mr. Ali Suleman Head-Faculty Affairs. EIT, Eritrea for their cooperation in bringing out this volume. I beg to acknowledge my sincere gratitude to my friend Shri S.K. Jha of Serials Publications, New Delhi for taking the responsibility of printing the book. I am also thankful to Shri K. Ravinder Reddy, NIRD for typesetting the book.

My special thanks are due to my wife Jagaddhatri and my son Tushar Subhra for their co-operation and constant support for the publication of this volume. I also express my heartfelt thanks to all my relatives, friends and well-wishers for their good wishes in bring out the volume.

Needles to say I am alone responsible for any error that may remain in the book.

**Shankar Chatterjee**

**In Loving Memory of Maternal Grand Parents**

**Maninadra lal Chakraborty**
**(Maternal Grandfather)**
**&**
**Ilabati Chakraborty**
**(Maternal Grandmother)**

**In Loving Memory of Paternal Grand Parents**

**Upendra Lal Chatterjee (Paternal Grand Father)**
**&**
**Kusum Kumari Devi (Paternal Grand Mother)**

# 1

## Islamic Public of Iran

It was April 2001, dated seventh, a fax message came to my Institute (National Institute of Rural Development, Hyderabad) from Islamic Republic of Iran (henceforth only Iran will be used), Ministry of Jihad for Agriculture. They want my presence in Tehran, as International resource person from India. From entire country, they selected me so naturally I was excited because if it materializes then it would be my first foreign visit (based on that day). Even if does not materialize, I wanted to take it sportingly as at the Grace of God, foreigners selected me. However, finally my first foreign visit materialized at the Grace of God (Mata Kamakhya). The Programme was on Training of Trainers Workshop on "Participatory Methods for Village Women in Small Scale Projects". It was a short duration Programme (held in May, 2001). The tour was sponsored by Food and Agriculture Organisation (FAO). As a part of the tour one day stay was made in Dubai. For this necessary arrangement was made by sponsored organization. Iran visit helped me to see two countries – Dubai and Iran. In 2001, there was no direct flight from Hyderabad to Dubai. My both ways journey-route were Hyderabad- Mumbai-Dubai-Tehran and vice-versa. My flight from Hyderabad to Mumbai was early morning of 10th May 2001. The previous night I did not have sound sleep as I was tensed, excited and cheerful. Everything went of well. When I landed Dubai it was night at about 7 P.M. (local time) of 10th May, 2001.

Dubai is a beautiful city. Its airport is very spacious. Terminal buildings are worthy to be seen. From 'Pin to Elephant' everything is available in the shops located in the airport with a reasonable rate. There are good numbers of restaurants in airport building itself. There are mosques – separately for men and women, telephone booths, etc. After completing all the formalities, I went to hotel where my stay was arranged. It was night at about 9.00 P.M., everywhere light and light. Vehicles are moving at a high speed on the roads. Roads are spacious, no digs and pits can be found any where. Next day morning my flight was for Tehran. So I didn't waste much time for dinner, I went to bed and had sound sleep. Next day when I reached Teheran, it was about 11 A.M. of local time. Journey was performed by U.A.E. flight, no doubt an excellent flight. One official from Ministry of Jihad for Agriculture came to receive me. My stay was arranged in a hotel. So when I reached there, it was about 1 P.M. In the same hotel one resource person from Pakistan and three resource persons from Europe as well as few Iranian participants who were from other provinces of Iran were also staying. Mention be made that except me, all other resource persons were female. But among the Iranian participants, few were male and rests female.

Pakistani resource person used to call me Bhai-saab and I used to call her Bahenji. We never felt that we were from different countries. We used to talk each other in Hindi. Before sharing my experience a few particulars about Iran are presented in the following Table.

## GEOGRAPHY

Iran, a popular name due to Persian civilization, lies in between Caspian Sea and the Gulf of Persian. It is in the central plateau surrounded by mountains. It is bounded to the north by the Republic of Turkmenistan, Russia, Azerbaijan and Armenia and the Caspian Sea; Afghanistan and Pakistan in the east, west by Iraq and Turkey and the south by the Persian Gulf and the Gulf of Oman. The central part of Iran and its eastern side is largely barren undulating desert. Its western side is having mountainous regions along with Iraqi and Turkish borders. In the north, the Albroz Mountains rise steeply from a fertile belt around the Caspian Sea.

**Table 1**

**Some basic particulars on Iran**

| *Sl No.* | *Particulars* | *Number/Value* |
|---|---|---|
| 1. | Total population (million) | |
| | (a) 1975 | 33.3 |
| | (b) 2004 | 68.8 |
| | (c) 2015 | 79.9 |
| 2. | Area | 1648000 sq.kms/636,296 sq. miles |
| 3. | Annual Population growth rate (%) | |
| | (a) 1975-2004 | 2.5 |
| | (b) 2004-15 | 1.4 |
| 4. | Urban Population (% of total population) | |
| | (a) 1975 | 45.8 |
| | (b) 2004 | 66.4 |
| | (c) 2015 | 71.9 |
| 5. | Population under age 15 (% of total) | |
| | (a) 2004 | 29.8 |
| | (b) 2015 | 25.6 |
| 6. | Population ages 65 & above (% of total) | |
| | (a) 2004 | 4.5 |
| | (b) 2015 | 4.9 |
| 7. | Population under nourished (% of total) 2001/03 | |

*Contd.....*

| *Sl No.* | *Particulars* | *Number/Value* |
|---|---|---|
| 8. | Human Development Index (HDI) (2004) | 0.746 |
| 9. | Life Expectancy at birth (2004) | 70.7 years |
| 10. | Adult Literacy rate (% 15+ years) 2004 | 77.0 years |
| 11. | Combined gross enrolment ratio for primary, secondary and tertiary schools (2004) (%) | 72 |
| 12. | (a) GDP per capita (PPPUS $) | 7525 |
| | (b) Per capita (US $) 2004 | 2439 |
| 13. | Population without sustainable access to an improved water source (2004) | 6 |
| 14. | Population below income poverty line (1990-2004) (%) | |
| | (a) 1 $ a day | 2 |
| | (b) 2 $ a day | 7.3 |
| | (c) National Poverty Line (1990-2003) | — |
| 15. | Population without sustainable access to an improved sanitation (%) | |
| | (a) 1990 | 17 |
| | (b) 2004 | — |
| 16. | GDP Per capita Annual Growth Rate (%) | |
| | (a) 1975-2004 | |
| | (b) 1990-2004 | (-) 0.1 (+)2.3 |

*Source:* Human Development Report, 2006

## CLIMATE

Like many countries in the world its climate also varies in different parts of the country. However, there are mainly four seasons in the country. In the summer, temperature in some parts goes up to even 40 Degree Celsius. Severe cold is observed in many parts during winter. Autumn and spring are other two seasons in the country. As a result of climatic conditions vis-à-vis it's seas and rivers, the country is enriched with various flora and fauna, many of which are rare varieties.

During my stay in Tehran, climate was very pleasant. Day time was little hot but night was cold. We all enjoyed the weather.

## FOOD

Iran is one of the few countries of the world which has a rich food culture. Its old civilization as well as availability of various natural produce (crops, fruits, vegetables, fish etc.), has been helping to develop varieties of food in the country. In India it is commonly told that "Persian dishes/ Iranian food". Iranian preparation is mouth-watering word for many Indians. However, my Iranian friends told that many fruits, vegetables and food items available in the world have originated from Iran. For example 'Kebab' has originated from Iran. Iranian caviar is a famous dish in the world. I had the opportunity to taste many Iranian dishes. As a part of the programme, everyday free lunch was provided in the hotel with different type of preparations.

Incidentally where we were staying arrangement of official lunch for all of us was made in the same hotel. Besides, our Iranian friends invited me and Pakistani friend almost every day for dinner. Many dishes were arranged. By seeing the dishes, my mouth watered – attractive looking and nice smell. In India there is a proverb in Sanskrit "Granena Ardhabhojona" (good smell means half eating), which I realised every lunch and dinner there. I was felling hungrier to see the food, so I relished. Iranians serve food in neat and clean way. Non-vegetarian dishes are sine qua non for invitees. I don't eat meat so every time fish was provided to me. I am fond of fish so I enjoyed. I still remember the fish fry which was once offered by our friends. The fish was about 200 grams in weight. By keeping the head (nicely cleaned) and main bone, fry was made with little spices in such a way that, at the prima–facie one may think it is a live fish.

Fry was so tasteful which many-a-times I narrated to my wife and relatives. My wife is also fond of fish so whenever I narrate to her she feels 'sorry' for not enjoying such preparation.

## LANGUAGE

Most widely spoken language is Persian (Farsi). Arabic is spoken in the North West of Iran. Turkish is spoken in the North West around Tarbriz. Educated persons know English. French and to some extent German and Italian are spoken by some business persons and officials. However, I have observed many words in Iran and India are common. Whenever I had gone to a hotel in the market for a cup of tea or coffee, many-a-times I heard "you are our Mehman so we will not take money". Mehman is also widely used in India. They have great likings towards Indians so many times the hotel owners declined to take money but I insisted and paid. Before going to Iran, I was in dilemma how to wish the people. In India we wish by uttering "Namaskar" or "Good morning". Of course, if I meet a Tamil friend in India, I wish by uttering "Onnakkam" and after that "Nalla Erekre Ingla". Similarly for a Telugu friend after `Namaskar', "Bagu Naara", Kannada "Chennagi Diya", Malayali "Sukha Manaye", Gujrati "Kem Cho", Assamese "Kene Achhe", Bengali "Kemon Achhen", Hindi speaking "Kaise Hai" or "Khabar Achhato" etc. In Iran I decided to wish by uttering, "Salam Alequm". They were responding me "Alequme Salam". I enjoyed this type of wishing. I got confidence also. I was saying – "Inshallah", "Massa Allah" and "Bismillahe Rahmane Rahim", according to the context. I observed people enjoyed many of them praised also. There is a recent research methodology known as Participatory Rural Appraisal (PRA). For rural development studies we use it. Under PRA basic philosophy is establishing rapport. For this we were taught to use local language or wishing people based on their culture or religion. I always follow this principal.

## RELIGION

Iran is the birth place of Zoroaster, one of the oldest prophets of the world. He was founder of Zoroastrian religion. However, presently 99.5 per cent of their populations are Muslim – mostly Shi'ite with a minority of Sunnis. The people of other religions include Christians, Jews and Zoroastrians.

Government

The Government of Iran is "Islamic Republic" which was founded after Islamic Revolution in 1979. Iran is divided into 28 provinces, 252 townships and 680 districts. Legislative power is vested with the Islamic Consultative Assembly (Majlis). The Majlis is represented by 275 members. President is the Chief Executive. He is elected by the people for four years. A twelve-member council of Guardians ensures that legislation is in accordance with the constitution and Islamic principles. Each province is administered by a Governor-General, each township by a Governor and each district by a Lieutenant-Governor.

The official flag of Iran is in tri colour – green, white and red colours with the sign of 'Islamic Republic of Iran'. The flag contains 22 marks depicting "Allaho Akbar" (God is great) inscribed on it.

In Iran all the persons have to follow two things as mentioned below. Violating any of these two issues is considered against social codes of behaviour:

(a) No consumption of alcoholic beverages
(b) Women must be suitably dressed and must wear a headscarf.

Besides the above, a male person cannot enter the room of a female person (friend etc.) and vice versa. If there is any work then they have to come outside the room. As mentioned already the hotel where I stayed our some Iranian friends (both male and female) hailing from other provinces also stayed, besides Pakistani friend (Bahenji). Our programme was about 400 meters away from the hotel. We all used to go together from the hotel but our meeting point was hotel lounge. We were never entering in each other room.

## CURRENCY

The currency of Iran is known as Iranian Rials. Both paper currency and coins are used. Paper currencies are in the denominations of 10000, 5000, 2000, 1000, 500, 200 and 100. On the other hand coins are in the denominations of 250, 100, 50, 20, 10 and 5. During the time of my visit 1 US Dollar was equal to 8000 Iranian Rials.

## TEHRAN

Tehran capital of Iran is one of the oldest cities in the world. It is neat and clean. Many multistoried buildings can be seen in the city. More number of four wheelers than two wheelers can be seen on the roads of the city. Tehran is Iran's capital city for more than 200 years. It is located in an altitude of 1200 meters high. Tehran is endowed with all the four seasons viz. autumn, spring, summer and winter. After being run over by the Mongols, the city was selected as capital of Iran and gradually developed in the late 18$^{th}$ century A.D. "Most of the historical buildings in Tehran were constructed in Qajar time". After Second World War, rapid development took place in Tehran. Today the city has modern hospitals, modern hotels, mosques, churches and synagogues for religious minorities, ski-slopes, all modern recreational services. Teheran's indoor grand bazaar is spread over to several kilometers housing thousands of shops. Even traditional items are available here. Tehran is famous for its museums. I was told that there were 26 museums, 20 public libraries, and more than 30 Universities and other higher educational institutions were located in and around Tehran. If one would like to visit all the museums than several days are required. My programme was for limited days that too after the daily schedule less time was available to visit museums etc. In spite of this, I visited few museums. The different museums depicted items used by different kings in different periods. Mention may be made here that civilization in Iran started in 3000 B.C. The chronology of different periods is represented below:

| | | |
|---|---|---|
| 3000 BC | – | 600 BC Elam (South-west of Iran) |
| 500 BC | – | 330 BC Achaemenian Empire |
| 330 BC | – | 220 BC Seleucids, Alexander's Successors |
| 220 BC | – | 220 AD Parthian Empire (Arsacid Dynasty) |
| 220 AD | – | 660 AD Sassanian |
| From 660 AD | | Moslem Conquest, Islamic period |

*Source:* "Parsa: Persepolis", 2000 by Werner Felix Dutz & Sylria A Matheson, Yassavoli Publications, Tehran.

There are altogether 6 major periods recorded in histories of Iran. However, according to the above mentioned publication, (Parsa: Parseplis) the periods mentioned above throws light about their regime with an approximate period. One can imagine exact time in B.C. or early A.D. is difficult to get. Even today many persons born 40-50 years back in India or other places cannot recall their date of birth.

However, the above publication has further mentioned that the origin of the Elamites and the other prehistoric settlers is not clear. The dynasties starting from Archaemenian rule and ending with the Arab Conquest were of Aryan origin.

A thorough look in the above periods vividly reveals that 26 museums in Tehran are the minimum requirement to accommodate for depicting the things available during the six major dynasties. Apart from museums, there are many other important places of interest in Tehran. These, inter alia, include Laleh Park, Albroz mountains, Azadi monument etc. Laleh Park is a park consisting of trees and plants. It is spread over to few kilometers. Laleh Park is considered as "lung" of Tehran, as it provides fresh oxygen to the residents of Tehran. I was really charmed to see the park. For me it looks like a mini forest. In the heart of the city existence of such park is fabulous. Credit goes to politicians, administrators, residents of Tehran city and others for not misusing/exploiting the park. Besides the park, mountains range is also another gift of nature. Tehran city is situated in a southern plain of Albroz mountains range. Its peak is covered by snow. The melting snow passes through the city for which open cemented wide drain has been constructed for continuous flow of water. Water flows through out the year. Mountains range, mini forest, flowing water etc made Tehran city a beautiful one. It seems nature has decorated the city in His/Her hand.

## PERSIAN NEW YEAR (NOROUZ)

During my stay in Iran many of my Iranian friends told about Persian New Year. They call it – Norouz. It is always celebrated on the first day of Farvardian, which corresponds with the 21 March every year. This day is celebrated in the country enthusiastically. A few lines about Norouz are mentioned here.

The New Year celebrations continue for about 15 days. It is believed that this New Year concept started in Iran about 3000 years back. During the course of celebrations, many customs and rituals are followed. Celebration is basically symbolic representation of two ancient concepts – End and Rebirth and Good and Evil. A few weeks before 21 March, every family germinates the seeds of barley, wheat or lentil as a symbol of renewal and good omen and to have fruits and crops throughout the year. Besides this, there are two other customs which symbolize the last days of the year. One is the "Shab-e Chahar Shanbeh Soury" (literally the eve of Red Wednesday), which is celebrated on the eve of the last Wednesday of the year. Bonfires are lit in public places and people leap over the flames, chanting "Sorkhie to azman o zardie man az to! (Give me your beautiful red colour and take back my sickly pallor!). Bonfires are lit at sunset to strengthen the consistency of light and warmth (symbols of good) and to neutralize darkness and cold. After leaping over the fires, an old clay pot which was used in the house during the year is filled with small stones and small objects which are no longer of use are brought out of the house and broken. When the clay pot breaks, one chants "Oh, pain and misfortune, keep away from our house, keep away poverty, sickness and evil omens from the house". On this occasion, people prepare and distribute sweets and a mixture of seven dried fruits and nuts known as "Ajeel-e Moshgel Gosha" (Get rid of difficulties) among the children.

Norouz also has many offerings to the spirits of the dead. On the last Thursday before the New Year, people visit the graves of their ancestors and pray for their dead ancestors and then distribute money, sweets or Halva (a kind of Saffron Cake) to the poor. In some places, people light lanterns and leave it on the graves of their ancestors.

Before the New Year everyone cleans their houses and decorates. Interestingly such practices prevail in India also. Before the New Year (different communities different dates in India), it is the ritual to clean their houses. Norouz is widely celebrated in Iran. All friends, relatives, guests and others participate in the celebration. They observe many rituals so it continues up to two weeks.

On the occasion of the Norouz, people take bath and wear new clothes. They believe New Year must be welcome with new and clean things. On that day, "Sofreh-e Haft Sinn" meaning 'the cloth of seven' is performed. Each household spreads a special cloth and on it seven symbols beginning with the letter "S": Sib (apples), Senjed (fruit of Jujube), Sekkeh (coin), Somagh (sumac), Sabzeh (sprouts), Serkeh (vinegar), Samanou (a dish made with germinated wheat ), or Sonbol (hyacinth) and Seer (garlic) are kept. The number "seven" is sacred number from ancient times in Persia. The other things placed on the cloth are the Holy Koran, a mirror, candles, and a bowl of water, goldfish, and painted eggs.

The family members sit around the "Sofreh-e Haft Sinn", waiting for the New Year. As the candles burn, the oldest person in the family reads verses of the Koran and at the stroke of Equinox, a verse is read which says: "Oh, you who change our hearts and sights, Oh, you who turn the nights to days and days to nights". The family members say "You change the fate and condition of man. Please change our lives and lead us to the best in life".

Every one exchanges gifts with friends and relatives. Sweets are eaten so that no bitter relationship develops in the New Year. The children receive gifts from the elders and grandmothers give grandchildren painted eggs. Moreover Norouz is the day when people forgive and forget grudges and past differences, and begin the new year with good thoughts, good words and good deeds. Thus 13 days pass in visiting friends and relatives. On the thirteenth day of Norouz, called "Sizdeh-Bedar", whole families leave their houses. They believe that staying at house on this day is not good. They take their sprouted seeds out of the house and proceed towards the parks and green fields to celebrate the rebirth of nature. They throw the sprouts into flowing water as an offering to complete the process of the end of one year and rebirth of a new year.

I was impressed when my friends lucidly narrated about Persian New Year (Norouz). Basic contents of the celebration still today have not been changed, al beit, it is celebrated for last 3000 years.

## VISIT TO MAZANDARAN PROVINCE

As a part of the programme, a visit was arranged in Mazandaran province, 250 kilometers away from Tehran. All the participants along with the resource persons went to study a poultry project located at Shahidabad village of Mazandaran. The project was sponsored by FAO for the benefit of the poor people. Based on the study I have published an article in Indian Economic Panorama, a journal published from New Delhi. This can be seen in Annexure-1.

A few lines about Mazandaran may be mentioned. Capital of Mazandaran is Sari, located about 250 kilometers away from Tehran. The province is spread over to an area of 24091 square kilometers with a total population of 26 lakh (1996 census). During the course of my visit in Mazandaran province, an incident happened which I will never forget in my life.

With our arrival at Shahidabad village, many children in the age group of 8 to 10 years came to meet us. They were curious to see so many foreigners. This is a common behahiour of the children. I am fond of talking to the children so I was just casually talking to them – names, school, classes etc. They felt very happy. I observed that they had lot of likings and regards towards Indians. Of course, Iranians like Indians very much. Iranian people commonly use the word, "Hindustan". They know many things about India like our president, prime minister, historical places of India etc. (Tajmahal, Agra Fort, Red Fort etc.). Even many persons know about caste system of India. Hindi movie is very popular. Many persons including army and police personnel told me the names of many Hindi movies. Few of them uttered dialogues from Hindi movies. The actors/actresses like Amitabh

Bachchan, Dharmendra, Shahrukh Khan, Hema Malini, Madhuri Dixit, and Rani Mukherjee were popular names in the country.

Let me come back to the children affairs. They were talking to me freely. I was enjoying. Suddenly I found one of them brought a cake (palm cake – 5/6 persons can eat) and requested me "sir, please you eat". I became emotional, eyes were full of water. I was thinking as a souvenir I must give something. Unfortunately, I did not have anything in my pocket. Whatever gifts I brought from India were in Tehran. I found some Indian rupees in my pocket. I gave the boy a ten-rupee note as souvenir vis-à-vis explained photograph of our `Father of the Nation' Mahatma Gandhi depicted in the note. He felt happy and with his happiness I was very satisfied. I extended my regret to other children as I could not give any type of souvenir to them. However, for the remembrance of the visit and incident, I took few group photos of the children. I always remember children are the manifesto of God because of their innocence. There is also an old Arab proverb that states, "Children are the reflections of their environment rather than their parents". I was recalling the proverb and thinking these children at this age having such a broad-mind because of their environment. Today's children are tomorrow's citizen and that is why Iran is fast developing. The country is self-sufficient in many respects. After completion of the study of poultry project we went to see Caspian Sea. It is located in Mazandaran province so arrangement was made to see Caspian Sea. I have seen all the seas of India so Caspian is not a new one for me. I observed some areas were marked as danger. Sea-beach is neat and clean. Many shops of food and gift items are located in the beach. We enjoyed with the food. I purchased some gift items. By looking at the Sea I was thinking what not God has created for mankind.

## SILK ROAD FROM HISTORICAL PERSPECTIVE

Many scholars and academicians told me about existence of "Silk Road". This is an important historical case, which helped to develop human civilization. There is a saying "road is a product of civilization". Naturally, I wanted to know more about "Silk Road". I collected some information about 'silk road'. A few lines in this regard are presented here. It is believed that the Road existed 2000 years back with 7000 kilometers long. This 'Road' not only connected the Eastern and Western civilizations but made economic-cultural transactions possible between the tribes residing in the Pacific Ocean, Indian Ocean and the Gulf of Persian on one side and Europe and northern Africa on the other. It is believed that during Sassanian period 'silk road' name was given. In that period, Iran was the center in which the rare merchandise such as silk, cotton materials, precious stones etc., from Central Asia; mirrors, Indian spices and fur from Caucasia, were traded.

Iranians first received and bought Chinese silk in its raw form or as weaved material, but later on decided to process the silk to suit according to their choice and culture. They created the silk materials with new colours and patterns. Famous silk design known as the "peacock's feather" became prevalent from the sixth century A.D. onwards.

Presently, measures have been taken to revive "Silk Road". For the Silk Road Project, the World Tourism Organisation (WTO), in collaboration with the Government of Islamic Republic of Iran and supported by the United Nations Educational, Scientific and Cultural Organization (UNESCO) have been organizing 'International Meeting' for revival of the 'Silk Road'. The countries, inter alia, include Azerbaijan, China, DPR Korea, Egypt, Georgia, Greece, India, Iran, Italy, Japan, Kazakhstan, Kyrgyzstan, Mongolia, Pakistan, Republic of Korea, Russia, Tajikistan, Turkey, Turkmenistan and Uzbekistan.

The Silk Road was not only economically important, it was a route through which knowledge was exchanged and civilizations were created. Saying is that "It was the identity of our ancestors who unanimously cooperated to leave us a message of peace and friendship." I was told that various tribes played important role in creating and maintaining this road according to their tastes and talents.

With the cooperation of the local tribes who lived near the Silk Road, the Iranians created all possible facilities which were necessary in safeguarding and creating safety on this important trading route. Water reservoirs, water wells, caravanserais, post stations, sentry posts, bridges and milestones were built and some parts of the roads were paved with flagstones.

After hearing and knowing the facts and figures of "Silk Road", I was thinking people of those days probably had a feeling of "Global Village". 'Oneness' concept might have generated in their mind in 2000 years back. Hope "Silk Road" will be revived for the benefit of the world. It is the reflection of a civilization.

## SOME HISTORICAL PLACES

Persian civilization is one of the oldest civilizations of the world, 3000 years old. Moreover the country is having three seas – Caspian Sea, Persian Gulf and Gulf of Oman vis-à-vis many rivers and mountains exist in Iran. Either from historical point of view or from tourist point of view, there are many places in the country. I stayed only for limited period so it was not possible to see all the places of interest. However, I tried to know some places of interest particularly from historical point of view, which are narrated here.

## SHIRAZ: UNIQUE DESIGN OF THE HOUSES

Shiraz is an old city. Its earlier name was Estakhr. This name can be found in the manuscripts of the Sassanid and Achaemenian period. The city got its importance from Islamic rule. It was reconstructed in 693 C.E. replacing ancient city of Shiraz (Estakhr). Ruins of old city of Shiraz reveal that it was surrounded by the walls from all its side having eight gates for entering in the city. All the houses in those days were divided in eleven residential districts.

Architectural design used in the old houses of the city was unique. Each house had two stone platforms installed on the sides of the entrance doorway. Each doorway also had an arch, which was decorated with coloured tiles. In many houses, entrances were decorated with tiles on which verses from Holy Koran were inscribed.

The entrance of the house would open into an aisle which leads to yard. Middle of each yard had a pond. Around the pond orchard trees and flower bearing plants were planted.

Houses were mainly of two types- building and common. Building type of house had stucco work mainly in the ceilings. Pictures of stucco work inter alia, included birds, bushes, angels, palm trees etc. Many house-owners painted these. In other words, those who had money could paint their houses. Some families put wooden panels to cover ceiling of the house. Another important characteristic was that each room in the house was used for specific purposes and had specific name. For example mirror room was the most beautiful room among the rooms of the house. Some persons covered all sides of inside of the room with mirrors. In some houses, the mirror room was partially covered. It means those who could afford it went for all sides mirror and those could not afford went for partial coverage. Name of other rooms were five-door room, seven-door room etc. Ventilation of the rooms were so scientifically designed that in winter rooms used to get plenty of sun-light and in summer (with the opening of doors) cool breeze passed through the rooms.

It has to be admitted that architecture of each of the house depicted scientific talent and caliber of the workers.

## SHUSHTAR: REVELATION OF HUMAN CIVILIZATION

Shushtar is located in Khuzistan province. Shustar is famous for its ancient civilization. Many man-made caves were discovered in the mountainous region of north-east of Shushtar. It is believed that these were built in Neolithic period.

One large fort "Fortress of Salasal" was discovered on the mountains of the southern part of the city. Ruins of the fort reveal that there were many gardens, barracks, stables, quarters, bathing place etc., in the fort. Construction of the fort was oval-shaped. Location of the fort was made in such a way that Karoun river can be seen from the fort, a well-planned fort. Arrangement for providing water to the dwellers of the fort was made meticulously. For this, a number of wells and canals were constructed.

Besides the above, ruins reveal that within the vicinity of Shushtar in those days dams and bridge on the river existed. All these evince the scientific knowledge and skill of the workers in ancient times.

## SUSA: ANCIENT CIVILIZATION

Various discoveries and relics evince that how people thought of their development in thousands years ago. It is believed that its civilization is one of the oldest civilizations in this earth.

Excavation by French archaeologists brought out many items belonged to historical period of Stone Age to

Fifth century A.H. (A.H. means After Hizri). Items inter alia, include beautifully painted pots etc. Ruins of many schools belonging to Second Millennium B.C. were discovered.

Many palaces and temples were discovered on the hill of Acropol with various inscriptions on it.

French archaeologist De Morgan appreciated ancient Susa for its planning and development.

## REY: CITY AS OLD AS BABYLON

It is an ancient city. Its old name is “Rega”. It is believed that the city is as old as Babylon.

Many potteries, vessels, stone pillars, and architectural works were discovered. Many of these belong to Fourth and Fifth centuries B.C. It is believed that city flourished in different periods of different kings but Moghuls ruined the city as they were invaders. Many relics which were later on discovered have been kept in museums of Iran and other countries.

## BISHABOUR: UNIQUE ARCHITECTURAL DESIGN

The ruins of the historical city at Bishabour were found 23 kilometers west of the city of Kazeroon. Many people throughout the year visit Bishabour. Architectural patterns of Bishabour are beyond imagination. The city was later called as “Antiuk Shapour” meaning very beautiful. Bishabour depicts a clear picture of Persian culture.

Archeological documents and scientific research vis-à-vis the works discovered in the city, speak the reality about how the city planning changed on the basis of political initiatives. During those days the city was the center of the ruling party where state directives and decrees were issued. Ruins of the city reveal that time to time new governments were established, economy flourished. Design of the city evinces that streets and roads cross each other in the city center. The streets and parks, other recreational centers, lush areas, and special complexes produced a beautiful design which contributed to the residents' tranquility.

The state buildings were constructed in the center of the old castle, north of the city. Each building in this complex had its own specifications and peculiarities.

The area had a temple known as Anahita temple. The temple is meant for Goddess of Water. Gigantic reception hall of the Shapour Palace, which was built in the southeastern part of the Anahita temple, covers about 781 square meters area. It is one of the earliest and biggest dome-shaped architectural works during the Sassanid period.

Bishabour's reception hall is comprised of four parallel and connected porches under a 25 meter high dome. The building itself is built in the shape of a cross with a total of 64 decorative niches.

There are beautiful paintings and stucco works in the palace. In the great Anahita Temple, site of building of Goddess of Water is another wonder that has been discovered in Bishabour.

This great cellar-like building is cube-shaped and has 14 meter long double –layer stone walls. No mortar has been applied in these walls. The width of the double layer wall is about 235 centimeters. On the side of the southern hall there are two doorways exclusively built for people to observe the flow of water. An area with dimensions measuring 27X23X7 cubic meters was dug in the depth of the ground for bringing Shapour River, 250 meters away from the temple. Thus river water flows near the temple.

The water distributing canals had been precisely designed and built to facilitate the flow of equal amounts of water in each of the waterways.

The great Bishabour temple, which was unearthed following scientific studies and archaeological excavations, is the symbol of a place designed to worship and admire water.

I was cherishing the sweet memories of all these. I was thinking if I would have stayed longer period in Iran, I could have seen many places.

## MY RETURN JOURNEY

My return journey was on 24th May. Many Iranian friends came to see off us. I had to purchase one suitcase in Tehran as almost all the participants gave me gifts – clothes, dry fruits, books, pens, metal box etc. Those who couldn't give came in the hotel/airport with the gifts. I was emotional for such love, affection and likings towards me. My Pakistani friend (Bahenji) was returning by the same flight. The flight was via Dubai. My destination was Hyderabad via Mumbai and for her Islamabad. We started morning from Tehran and reached before noon to Dubai. For both of us about 8 hours stay in Dubai. Her flight was little earlier than me. This time outside going was not allowed as we did not have transit visa for eight hours. We spent the time in the airport itself. Based on our tickets we have eaten foods in the airport as there are 8 – 10 hotels/restaurants in the airport including Indian restaurants. Since we were two so how the time passed we could not imagine. Announcement was made for Islamabad flight. She left with heavy heart. I was also sad as I would not be able to meet Bahenji in future easily, because on 14th August 1947 one part of India has become Pakistan – a foreign country for us. About half-an-hour later announcement for my flight was made. Flight took off at night, mid-night's Dubai, a city dressed with colourful lights, a beautiful view. Slowly lights of the city faded. I could understand we were near to the "Twinkle Twinkle Little Star".

## REFERENCES

'Iran at a Glance', 1998, Iran, Tehran.

"Parsa: Persepolis", 2000 by Werner Felix Dutz & Sylria A Matheson, Yassavoli Publications, Tehran.

"Silk Road", 1997 GAM Publishing, Tehran.

**IRAN**

**A view of the Class Room.**

**A view of Tehran Fity**

**Azadi Monument in Tehran**

**Author and Pakistani Resource Person (Near Azadi Monument)**

**Author with the Participants**

**Author with his Iranian Friend in Tehran City**

**Graves of the Soldiers of Shahidabad Village Killed in Iraq War**

**Photographs depicting Soldiers Killed in Iraq War near the Graves (Shahidabad Village)**

**Caspian Sea**

**Laleh Park**

**Author with the Participants in PRA Exercise**

**A view of the Building of Telefood Project funded by FAO**

**Participants carrying out PRA Exercise**

**Villagers near the Building of Telefood Project**

**Villagers of a village of Mazandaran Province**

**Children of a village of Mazandaran Province. They Offered Cake to the Author**

# 2

## The State of Eritrea

My second visit was in of the State of Eritrea (henceforth only Eritrea will be used), a country located in northeast of Africa. I was selected for the post of Associate Professor in Economics by the Professors of Eritrea who conducted interview in India. Interview was held in 2004 in few major cities of our country. As mentioned in Iran chapter I am working in Hyderabad office of National Institute of Rural development (Government of India), so I appeared in Hyderabad. The post is meant for a newly established Institute of Eritrea, known as Eritrea Institute of Technology (EIT). It was set up in 2004. So before our batch another batch of teachers mostly from India were recruited. I was naturally delighted (only person selected for the post of Associate Professor in Economics in our batch) when I came to know about my selection. I extended my heart-felt thanks to God. It was for two years contract. My Institute allowed me to join in Eritrea retaining lien. I am grateful to the then Director General of National Institute of Rural Development, Shri Lalit Mathur, IAS, who as per rules allowed me. Institute also allowed me to retain my residential quarter, as my wife and son would stay back in India. My son that time was in 10$^{th}$ class of CBSE.

It was 10$^{th}$ February 2005 I reached at Hyderabad airport. Global Placement organization of Hyderabad arranged our ticket (Received from Eritrea). Entire selection in India was held under the aegis of Global

Placement. My wife and son were little upset as my stay in Eritrea was for two years.

We about 55 Indians from different parts of the country finally met at Mumbai international airport for our departure to Asmara (capital of Eritrea). Yemeni Airlines flight started evening from Mumbai and at midnight of 11th February 2006 we reached at Asmara international airport. Eritrean officials of Ministry of Education came to receive us. With the completion of all custom formalities when we came out from airport it was 2 A.M of 11th February 2005. Outside temperature might be 3-4 Degree Celsius, severe cold. Of course we were informed earlier about all these so we wore sweater/jacket. We were accommodated in different hotels. I along with my one friend of Maharastra (Mechanical Engineer) was put in Nyala Hotel. It is under Ministry of Tourism, Eritrea. We about 20 persons were accommodated in this hotel. In our previous batch (1 year early) also those who came many of them (around 20) were staying in the hotel voluntarily. So it was a mini India in the hotel itself. They arranged separate cooking in a common kitchen of a room in the hotel, which was arranged by the management of the hotel. So cooking was not the problem for us. I am fond of cooking and for this I was awarded by The Deccan Chronicle and The Times of India (Hyderabad edition) for recipe writing. I brought minimum cooking utensils including a pressure cooker. My roommate was helping me in cooking process. It was a great help for me. I personally feel if things are ready then cooking is not a problem. After 10 days of rest finally our work started at EIT. It is located at about 20 kilometers away from the city. For us separate transport was arranged so going and coming was not the problem. Otherwise it is difficult to go 20 kilometers as transport system is not well developed.

**Independence of Eritrea:** Eritrea is young nation got its independence on 24 May 1991. Although it was declared independent country through a UN supervised referendum held in April 1993. The country celebrates its independence every year on 24 May.

**About EIT:** After independence government took several steps to develop education particularly higher education in Eritrea. Establishing Eritrea Institute of Technology (EIT) in 2004 is one of the major steps. In EIT apart from teaching of engineering and science subjects other subjects including social science, fine arts, physical education etc are taught at pre-degree and degree level. It is exclusively under the Ministry of Education, State of Eritrea. Mainly an academician who has been designated as Vice-President, Academic Affairs, heads EIT. During my tenure, Vice-President was an Eritrean, Dr. Ghebreberhan Ogubazghi. He has done his Ph.D in Electrical Engineering from France. The other management staff includes both Eritreans and Indians. Next to Vice-President is Chairman, Council of Deans. The post was held by Prof G. Ramana Rao from Andhra Pradesh. A few of others who were holding important positions include Prof. T. Bose Babu, Director Examinations & Evaluations from Andhra Pradesh, and Prof. L. Ashraf Ali Khan, Dean, College of Social Science from Chennai.

EIT fortnightly publishes a newsletter under the banner of Horizon. Its editor is an Indian hails from Jammu and Kashmir, Dr. Ashaq Malik. Dr. Malik besides his teaching work looks after timely bringing out the newsletter. Due to his sincere effort last two years the newsletter is being regularly published on time. The newsletter gives lot of information about the latest science related activities happening in the world apart from Institute's activities.

## BRIEF HISTORY OF ERITREA:

Since Eritrea is not widely known to Indians so I would like to mention detail about Eritrea including its history.

History of Eritrea is very old. One of the reasons is that Eritrea is located near the Red Sea. As we know any human settlement develops near sea or river. That way longback human settlement started in Eritrea. The history of Eritrea throws light in this regard. Here few points are highlighted. This part of the history of Eritrea has been collected from different sources viz., "Eritrea, Come, Fall in Love (2005)", "The World Book (1994)", "Industrial Statistics 2004" and different text books on history of Eritrea. People inhabited in Eritrea since Eighth century B.C. The first inhabitants were Nilotic people from the Nile. "The Cushites arrived with successive waves of Hamitic stock and the Southern Arabian Tribes introduced the Semitic culture". (Eritrea: 2005). It is believed that Semitic language evolved into Geez from which Tigrigna and Tigre originated. In the 4$^{th}$ century A.D., Christianity spread to Eritrea. In the early Islamic period, the trail of Sahaba was established when a group of Mohammed's companions (Sahaba) came from Mecca to Massawa and hinterland to escape persecution. The Aksum kingdom became the first important state in the area around 50 A.D. The kingdom reached greatest power in between 300's and 600's A.D. The coastal region of Eritrea came under the rule of Ottoman Empire in the 1500's. About the same time kings from Ethiopia and Sudan tried to capture rest of Eritrea. In the 1800's Egypt, France, and Italy tried to control Eritrea. In 1882, Italy occupied the port of Assab. In 1885 Italy occupied port of Massawa and other regions along the coast. By 1889 Italy had conquered all of Eritrea. Italy used Massawa as a base for an invasion of Ethiopia. Ethiopian Emperor Menelik II defeated Italian forces in 1896. But Italian conquered Ethiopia in 1935. During Second World War British forces defeated Italians in 1941 and British rule was established. They ruled up to 1952. It was later on made an autonomous unit federated with Ethiopia and then annexed with

Ethiopia in 1962. In 1962 Ethiopia declared Eritrea to be a province of Ethiopia. In the meantime civil war broke out. In 1974 following a major famine in Ethiopia the military rulers of Ethiopia seized the government and removed the then King Haile Selassie. They established a temporary government called the Dergue. Finally in 1991 after 30 years of armed struggle with Ethiopia, Eritrea became an independent nation.

During Italian rule Italy restricted education among Eritreans. An Eritrean could study up to primary grade beyond that s/he was not allowed. Italians wanted Eritrean should be soldiers, telegraph operators, typists, household workers etc. However, during British rule education was improved. Many schools were established.

Italian colonization in Eritrea reveals that it helps to develop some industrial units. They established number of manufacturing units in between 1887 and 1930. These manufacturing establishments were classified in 15 groups viz., pasta making, button making, flour milling, salt manufacturing etc. During this period there was a substantial growth in public investments of which a significant portion was deployed in establishment such as tanneries, textile mills, electrical workshops etc. Again when Italian rule was replaced by British rule for a period of 5 months many of the industrial units were closed. However, after 5 months these were revived. After 1943 industrial production started falling due to closer of some units. In 1946 British began to dismantle or sale many factories and projects established by the Italians. For example British sold airport of Asmara and Assab to other countries; sold Asmara-Massawa ropeways (cableways) to other countries; salt factory to Yemen; floating docks of Massawa to Pakistan. It is reported that the British removed or sold an estimated 86 Million Pound worth of industrial plants and equipments to other countries. During Ethiopian rule (1961-1991), Ethiopia followed industrial policies that were hostile to Eritrea's economic growth. As a result the expansion of existing industries and establishment of new ones were totally discouraged. During Dergue regime (1975-1991) also, a deliberate policy of destroying was pursued. All major establishments were under state ownership. The planning and marketing activities were subject to centralized control and direction. After independence the Government of Eritrea inherited 42 public and 645 private manufacturing units, which were almost in dormant conditions.

## SOME BASIC PARTICULARS ON ERITREA:

Eritrea is a country located at extreme North East of Africa. Total land area of Eritrea is about 125,000 Square Kilometers (Eritrea: Ministry of Tourism, 2003). On the other hand, the World Bank data reveal that its geographical area is118, 000 square kilometers. So there is little controversy about its area. In the absence of population census (now under way), its population figure also varies. As per the report of Eritrea Basic Education Statistics, 2002, its population was 3.2 million with average density of population 29 persons per square kilometer. On the other hand, World Bank statistics on population show that in 2002, population was 4 million. After the population census the picture will be clear in this regard.

Eritrea lies in between 12° and 18° North latitude and 36° and 44 ° East longitudes. The country is having more than 1000 Kilometers of coastal line along the Red Sea with about 350 off shore islands. Besides Red Sea, which is located east and Northeast side of Eritrea; it shares boundaries with Sudan in the North and West and Ethiopia and Djibouti in the South.

The name Eritrea has been derived from the ancient Greek word 'Red' named after 'Erythrean Sea' i.e., Red Sea. The country is having six provinces/regions, locally known as Zoba, 57 sub-Zobas/sub-regions and 2606 villages. The names of Zobas are: Maekel, Anseba, Debub, Gash Barka, Southern Red sea, and Northern Red sea. Some basic particulars of Eritrea may be seen in Table-1

**Table 1**

**Some basic particulars on Eritrea**

| Item | Particulars |
|---|---|
| 1. Population (millions) | |
| (a) 1975 | 2.1 |
| (b) 2002 | 4.2 |
| (c) 2015 | 5.8 |
| 2. Annual growth rate of Population (%) | |
| (a) 1975–2004 | 2.4 |
| (b) 2004–2015 | 2.9 |
| 3. Urban Population (% of total) | |
| (a) 1975 | 13.5 |
| (b) 2004 | 19.0 |
| (c) 2015 | 24.4 |
| 4. Illiteracy (% of people 15 & above) | |
| (a) Male | 42 (1990) & 33 (1999) |
| (b) Female | 72 (1990) & 61 (1999) |
| 5. Population without sustainable access to improved sanitation (%) 2004 | 91 |
| 6. Population without sustainable access to an improved water resource 2004 | 40 |
| 7. GDP (US billions $) | |
| (a) 2002 | 0.6 |
| (b) 2003 | 0.9 |
| 8. GDP per capita (US $) | |
| (a) 2002 | 150 |
| (b) 2003 | 190 |
| (c) 2004 | 219 |
| 9. GDP (per capita % growth 1990-2004) | 0.8 |

*Contd....*

| Item | Particulars |
|---|---|
| 10. GDP per capita (PPPUS $ 2004) | 977 |
| 11. National Poverty Line (1990-2003) (%) | 53 |
| 12. Population under 15 years (% of total) | |
| (a) 2004 | 44.8 |
| (b) 2015 | 42.6 |
| 13. Population 65 years & above (% of total) | |
| (a) 2004 | 2.3 |
| (b) 2015 | 2.6 |
| 14. Population under nourished (% of total)2001-03 | 73.0 |
| 15. Human Development Index (2004) | 0.454 |
| 16. Life Expectancy at Birth (2004) | 54.3 Years |

*Source:* Compiled from

(i) Human Development Report 2006, UNDP

(ii) World Development Indicators, World Bank, 2005

(iii) The Little Data Book 2001, The World Bank.

The topography of the country is very diverse, with its scenic beauty making up one of the country's most important attractions. Its landscape also greatly influences the climatic pattern of the country. Asmara is the capital of Eritrea located at about 2450 meters high than the sea level so weather of Asmara is pleasant through out the year. The currency of Eritrea is known as Nakfa, 1 US dollar is equal to 15 Nakfa approximately.

## LANGUAGE

There are nine ethno linguistic groups in Eritrea. The working languages are mainly Tigrigna, Arabic, and English. Besides Tigrigna and Arabic, seven other languages are spoken in the country. Geez language is the mother of Tigrignna language. Geez is also a calendar, which is followed in many parts of Eritrea and Ethiopia.

The community and languages are presented below.

| Community | *Language* |
|---|---|
| Afar | *Afar* |
| Bilein | *Bilein* |
| Hedareb | *Hedareb* |
| Kunama | *Kunama* |
| Nara | *Nara* |
| Rashaida | *Arabic* |
| Sahoo | *Sahoo* |
| Tigre | *Tigre* |
| *Tigrigna* | *Tigrigna* |

I am fond of learning and speaking languages. I took interest to learn Tigrigna which is widely spoken in Eritrea. I was told people of all the nine communities along with their mother tongue know Tigrigna. I observed whenever I was speaking Tigrigna people enjoyed. I should mention here that in Tigrigna, for male and female different words are used. For example "how are you" in Tigrigna, means "Keme Allakha" (for male) and "Keme Allakhee" (for female). Similarly for the word 'please', it is "Bejahkha" (for male) and for female "Bejahkhee". Some other words are 'take' means "Inka" (male) and "Inkee" for female. Sit down means "Kofbel (male) and "Kofbelee" (female) etc. Every time they use the word 'please' i.e. "Bejahkha"/ "Bejahkhee".

## RELIGION

People are broadly divided in to two religious groups – Christian and Muslim. The population of the high plateau is predominantly Christian. On the other hand, population in the low land and coast are predominantly Muslim.

## MY EXPERIENCE ON CHRISTMAS CELEBRATION

Every year on 7th January Christmas is celebrated in Eritrea. Variation of date is due to different calendar followed by Eritrean as most other parts of the world Christmas is celebrated on 25th December. In each zoba and sub zoba, Government sponsored programs are held on 7th January. In 2006, venue for celebrations was our Institute. Each year different venues are selected in each sub-zoba. For the celebrations, invitations were extended to many VIPs including faculties of our Institute. Since EIT is located about 20 kilometers away from Asmara city so vehicles were arranged. Among the Indian teachers many did not turn up from India (after vacation) so we the Indians were approximately 15 in number attended. Many of us went about 11.30 AM. By this time lunch was arranged (buffet). Many vegetarian and non-vegetarian dishes were prepared. After lunch cultural programs started, that included songs, music and dance. Many of our Indian friends also participated. Free beer was served. We enjoyed Christmas in different environment and on different date.

## EXPERIENCE ON EPIPHANY DAY:

Every year 19 January is celebrated as Epiphany Day. I was told Jesus was baptized on this day. It is a national holiday. Thousands of people having Christian faith gather in a place. The Bishop sprinkles holy water on the head of each person. The people celebrate with full honor and gaiety. They prepare varieties of foods in their house and invite guests. An Eritrea family invited me for a cup coffee in the evening. They prepare coffee powder in their house by grinding coffee seeds. The coffee powder is mixed with hot water which is boiled in charcoal stove. Every time after serving black coffee the pot is put on the charcoal stove. Thus hot coffee is served 3-4 times to each person. For me, the host arranged along with coffee some items like popcorn, barley-grain fry, biscuits etc. I enjoyed the coffee ceremony.

## EID CELEBRATIONS: MY EXPERIENCE

The celebration of EID in Eritrea is just like India. Only dates vary from India 1-2 days. During Ramadan month, Muslims observe fasting at daytime. On the day of Eid-Al –Fetir people pray at the mosques. On 23rd October 2006 Eid-Al-Fetire was celebrated in Eritrea. On this day the prayer headed by Shiek Salim Ibrahim from office of the Eritrean Mufti was conducted. Ministers, Government officials, diplomats and invited guests as well as thousands of people attended at Bahti Meskerem square (main city area) for the prayer. In a speech delivered by Sheik Salim outlined the importance of religious event. He also stressed to support the families of martyrs.

On the occasion of Eid, Muslims invite guests in lunch or dinner. In one Eid occasion a family invited me for coffee. It was home made coffee. Coffee was prepared in the earthen pot and served in a small cup number of times. Along with the coffee, some snacks were also arranged. Mention may be made here that both the Eids and Prophet Mohammad's birthday are celebrated widely in Eritrea. All these occasions are national holidays.

## CLIMATE

Eritrea can be divided into three major climatic zones-central highlands, coastal region, and western low lands. In the central high land area, climate through out the year is pleasant as it varies from 0 Degree to 26 Degree Celsius. Temperature in the coastal region varies widely – June to September is extremely hot with daily temperatures ranging in between 40 Degree and 50 Degree Celsius and in winter it varies from 21 Degree to 35 Degree Celsius. The Western low land is also having almost similar climate like coastal zone. The central highlands are densely populated and intensively cultivated by settled farming. Most of the coastal plains have limited fertile area for doing agriculture. The

Western low lands are having fertile land with irrigation facilities.

## CULTURE AND TRADITION

Handshake is a common practice in Eritrea irrespective of gender consideration. It is ritual to shake hands with everyone whether all know the person or not, when someone enters in a room. It was observed that if someone visits other's house and the person may be busy with cooking, gardening etc., the culture was extending wrist to the visitor(s). Visitor touches the wrist. Besides, among the close relationship 'shoulder bump' is common. Both the person clasp right hands together bump each other shoulders three times. Another way of greetings among the close relationship is cheek-to-cheek touching; irrespective of gender, one puts his/her cheek to other. The process continues three to five times.

## CELEBRATION OF GEEZ NEW YEAR

In many parts of the Eritrea, 11$^{th}$ September is celebrated as New Year based on Geez calendar. The day is observed as national holiday. People wear new dresses, ladies wear their ornaments, eat special foods. On this day in many houses cattle, sheep, goats etc are slaughtered. Many Eritrean friends told me that in any major celebrations slaughtering of animal is must. If income of a person is more then cattle is slaughtered otherwise sheep/goat or chicken. I was told beef was costlier than mutton. Mutton is costlier than fish. I am fond of fish so I enjoyed fresh fish of Red Sea.

## DINNING

Eritrean style of eating is different than Indian eating system. Most meals are eaten together in one big plate by hand. This practice is followed either in family or in any function. The plate is kept in a low table.People sit around the plate. Normally *Injera* (a big size looks like our Dosa, at a time 3-4 persons can eat) made of local cereal known as *taff* is eaten with sauce, vegetables, meat etc. After initial taste (first taste) guest should say 'tu'um', meaning delicious (if any guest(s) is invited). This is nothing but showing respect and appreciation to the members of the household. During eating, right hand is used and fingers should not touch lips. Before the meal, homemade drink locally known as *swa* is served .Serving *swa* is common in the marriage and other festivals Sometimes after meal coffee is served to the guests. Coffee seeds are purchased from the market. They roast coffee-seeds in the house and then grind it. Local coffee pots made of clay are used for preparation of coffee.

## VISIT TO MARKETS: MY OBSERVATIONS

Dinning is associated with markets as things are available only in the market. I stayed for two years so I closely observed goods available in the markets of Asmara.

(a) **Fish:** In Asmara only Red Sea fishes are available that comes mainly from Massawa port (more than 100 kilometers away). No river or pond fish is available in Asmara. In spite of existence of Red Sea, availability of fish in Asmara is uncertain. In other words every day, fish is not available. Two main reasons have been cited for this. First is Eritreans like meat than fish. Secondly, bringing fish sometimes is a problem as fish is available only in Massawa. Massawa is a very hot place. However, I have to admit Red Sea fishes are very tasteful. One of the reasons stated for this is that, like many other seas, Red Sea in this part is not polluted. Some of the tasteful fishes, inter alia, include, King fish, Queen fish amd Barakunda. Besides Red Sea fish, tin-fish is available through out the year in all grocery shops, and super markets. Two varieties of tin-fishes are available – Sardine and Tuna.

(b) **Vegetables and fruits:** Through out the year many vegetables are available in Asmara. These inter alia, include potato, onion, tomato, cabbage, pumpkin, salad-leaf and a local variety of cucumber (locally known as Jukni). The other vegetables like cauliflower; bringal, radish etc. are available in limited shops. Vegetables like bitter gourd and gourds are not available. The vegetables that are available are very fresh and tasteful. Fruits like mousambi (a type of orange) and banana are available in plenty in all shops (vegetables and grocery) through out the year. Besides, seasonal fruits like watermelon and B*alaas* (Cactus fruit) are available in the seasons.

(a) **Cereals:** Rice is not very popular among Eritreans, but foreigners prefer it. Rice is imported mainly from Pakistan and Thailand; lentils of many varieties are grown in Eritrea. Edible oils are imported.

(b) **Clothes and shoes:** There are sufficient numbers of cloth and shoe shops in Asmara. Although shoes to some extent are made in Eritrea but clothes mainly come from china and other countries.

(c) **Electronics and other goods:** Almost all the electronic goods are imported from different countries. In fact there are no manufacturing units of electronic goods in Eritrea. Stationery goods like paper, pen, pencil etc, are also imported. Goods like salt, toilet soap, washing soap, dish-cleaning detergents etc are produced locally vis-à-vis imported to some extent.

## IMPORTANT PRODUCE OF ERITREA

The country produces many agricultural goods. Some of these are barley, lentils, millet, sorghum, wheat, dairy products, vegetables and fruits. Another important cereal that is widely grown and eaten is *Taff*. The other important activity is animal husbandry. Herders raise cattle, goat and sheep.

Eritrea mainly exports live animal and hides and skins. Studies reveal that Eritrea is having deposits of mineral resources like crude oil, gold, copper, zinc, potash and iron ore (Ministry of Information, 2002). But due to border dispute with Ethiopia, exploitation is not presently undertaken.

## NAME OF THE PEOPLE AND MARRIAGE

Names of the people of christian faith are either drawn from Bible or local names. In case of Muslims, names are Arabic origin. Muslim names are commonly found in India also. A person is having his/her first name, then father name. In other words, all sons and daughters second name is father's name. Every one is called by his/her first name only. In case of women even after her marriage name is not changed. Original name is retained.

Christian marriages are performed normally on Saturdays or Sundays. However during fasting days before Easter no marriages are performed. Bridegrooms wear full suit and brides wear white gown. The gowns are costly so many poor persons borrow it from the shops. Muslims marriages are held at any time in a year, normally during Ramadan month, it is avoided.

## VISIT TO A MARRIAGE CEREMONY OF TWIN BRIDES

During my two years stay in Eritrea, I attended 10-12 marriages. My experience on twin marriages is explained. On 19th February 2006, I attended the marriage. Mother (a widow) is having three sons and three daughters. Her husband and another son died in Ethiopia war, in two different periods. One son and one daughter already got married. Of the three daughters the marriage celebration is for two daughters both are twin. Both of them work in Health Department of Eritrea. Wedding was over on 18th February and 19th was party where friends and relatives were invited. Generally lunch is offered to the guests on occasion of marriage. Here also it was lunch. I went around 12 noon. Just near the house a tent was erected where people sat. Many invitees came by this time and food simultaneously was served - *Injera* and beef. In a low-lying table a big plate was kept where 3-4 persons were eating. About 8 to 10 tables were kept and at a time 30-40 persons were eating. As already mentioned *Injera* is made out of a cereal known as *Taff,* which is widely grown in eastern part of Africa. It is fermented and prepared. It is staple food in Eritrea. Many families keep for 3-4 days after preparation. Mostly in the marriages *Injera* and beef are served.

Before serving the lunch, home made local drinks *Swa* was served. It is also brewed of a cereal and having mild effect on the body. Generally in the marriages *Swa* is served. People consume 3-4 full glasses at a time. I tasted *Swa*. Since I do not take any type of meat so I was offered *Injera*, rice, potato fry and vegetables. I was told that these were prepared for bride and bridegrooms and close family members. In one corner of the tent a professional singer was singing and another one was playing piano. I enjoyed the music and songs al beit, all these were in *Tigrigna.* Around 2 PM foods were served to brides and bridegrooms. They were sitting on four special type of decorated chairs placed on Dias. After the food, cakes were brought. The cakes about 10 in number (each weighting 1-1.5 kilograms) were kept on different sides of a big stand, which almost looks like a tree. With starting of music, the brides and bridegrooms also started dancing. With the continuation of dancing each one (only brides and bridegrooms) was cutting the cake and putting to other's mouth. We were observing. Music was in full volume. Mother and brother of the brides also came and put a portion of cakes to brides and bridegrooms. The process continued for about 40 minutes. Remaining cakes were taken inside the house. Functions were over, brides and bridegrooms left for the in-laws' house with the vehicle exclusively arranged for them.

## VISIT TO A SILVER JUBILEE MARRIAGE INVITATION

It was January 14, 2006. The entire India celebrates *Pongal, Makad Sankranti and Bhogali Bihu* but I enjoyed in different way. I was invited by an Eritrea family to attend their silver jubilee marriage celebration. The family know me last one year. It was lunch invitation. I was only Indian among the invites of about 250 persons. They felt very happy to see me and introduced some of their grown up children. The bride and groom sat on two decorated chairs placed on a Dais. All the guests greeted them. Many types of foods were prepared including vegetarian and non-vegetarian. It was buffet. I enjoyed the vegetarian food. This time I found along with *Swa* another local house made drink known as *Abake* was prepared. I tasted *Abake*, it is little sweet in taste, and *Swa* is little sour in taste. Both *Swa* and *Abake* are having mild effect on the body. It does not lead to any giddiness like other hard drinks.

## MY EXPERIENCE ON INDEPENDENCE DAY CELEBRATION

On 24th May 2005 I could enjoy the independence day of a foreign country. As already mentioned Eritrea was liberated from Ethiopia on 24th May 1991. About one week before the Independence Day, celebrations started with tableau, processions, and patriotic songs. School children of different ages with colourful dresses spontaneously participated. All roads and private buildings were decorated with colourful lights. The flags were hoisted in all the private and government buildings, shops and offices. On 23rd night 2005 in each and every corner of the streets cultural programmes were organized. Thousands of persons irrespective of age and sex came out to the street. Exactly at 12.00 midnight sky was full of lights due to different type of fire-works. Bars were crowded with the people. Since 14 years back Eritrea was liberated so many Eritreans have seen the gloomy days of colonial rule. Many freedom fighters and others explained me how they suffered during freedom struggle. They enjoy wholeheartedly their independence day. I was born much later than our independence so I always enjoyed the taste of independence in my country. However this time in a foreign country, I enjoyed their independence in different environment.

## MY OBSERVATIONS ON MARTYRS' DAY AND ARMED STRUGGLE DAY

### Martyrs' Day

The martyrs' day is observed every year on 20th June. I had the opportunity to observe this event on 20th June 2005. On the evening of 19th June 2005, thousands of people came out from their houses. Everyone was moving through the main street with lightened candles holding in their hands. On this occasion no streetlights were lit. The people assemble in the main square of Asmara city. The President of Eritrea addressed to the nation in memory of martyrs'. Prayers were held by the people of both the religions. Patriotic songs were performed for inculcating patriotic feelings among the people. On 20th June all Eritreans visit cemeteries of martyrs' and also observe fasting upto1P. M. All bars remain closed both on 19th and 20th June. Mentioned may be made here that about 65000 persons lost their lives for the 30 years of freedom struggle and another 19000 persons died to protect the independence of Eritrea. (Eritrea Profile, June 22, 2005).

### Beginning of Armed Struggle day

Every year 1st September is celebrated as Armed Struggle day. Freedom struggle started against the regime of Ethiopia on this day. It started from Gash Barka region with the sacrifice of life of Mohammed Faid (Eritrea Profile, 13th May 2006). It is a national holiday. The people of Eritrea greatly remember as from this day onwards freedom fighters started fighting not against enemies but even hazardous situation. In this regard the Eritrea Profile, only English news paper of Eritrea, may be quoted, "The Eritrean fighter fought not only against human enemies but against nature; the torrid deserts of Sahel, burning sandstorms, poisonous snakes and scorpions, hunger, thirst, and all sorts of battle hazards".

### Celebration on Meskal day (Finding of True Cross of Jesus Crucifixion)

Meskal is very popular word for the Christians of Eritrea. It is celebrated every year on 25 September. Initially I did not know significance of Meskal. Later on I came to know that on this day Cross of Jesus Christ was found. Meskal is a local word meaning finding of True Cross (crosses on which Jesus Christ was crucified). Next to Easter, Meskal is greatly celebrated by the Christians of Eritrea. On the occasion of both Easter and Meskal, people pray, slaughter animals and eat varieties of foods. Many families invited me, on these days for a cup of coffee. Our Indian friends of Christian faith told me that in India it was not widely celebrated.

## Places for the Visitors

There are number of places for the visitors in Eritrea. Asmara, capital itself is a place endowed with many tourist spots. Some important sites of Asmara are presented below.

## Sites at Asmara

The present capital of Asmara was built by Italy during 1890 to 1940 as during that period time-to-time Italians developed Asmara. It is located at about 2450 meters height from the sea level so through the year climate is very pleasant. Asmara is having good hotels. With very low crime rate in entire Eritrea, tourists are relieved of any tension. The important places of interest in Asmara include the following.

*The Church of our Lady of the Rosary (The Cathedral)*

Asmara is very popular for the Church of our Lady of the Rosary, popularly known as the Cathedral. Till 1993 it was the Church of Apostolic Vicar of Eritrea and then of the Apostolic Administrator of Eritrea. The present building of the Church was constructed in 1923 and in the same year it was blessed. Before that there was a small church, which was constructed in 1895, but after demolishing it, the present one has come up.

The Church has a central nave, two aisles, and a transept. It is 40 meters long, and its highest height is 25 meters. The Church is topped with a bronze statue of St. Michael the Archangel. Internally it is decorated with array of illumination. There are eight artistic bells on the tower. Weight of the biggest bell is 83 quintals. Other buildings of the Church inter alia, include the theatre with 500 seats, the Friary, printing press, Catholic Institute of Theology, kindergarten school etc. The Church may be considered as the "main lung" of the social life and religious activities of Asmara city. It is the oldest among the Catholic Churches of Asmara. Few occasions I visited the church, it is really beautiful. Every time, I prayed my own way sitting in one corner of the bench - a different environment, a different situation. I believe God is one, only means of praying is different. Ultimately we all pray to God.

*Jamle at Khulafa's el Rashedin Mosque:*

The mosque was built in 1938.There is large square area in front of the mosque where Friday prayers are held. The stone used in the construction of mosque was light colored. It is really attractive.

*Tank Graveyard:*

The military tanks, armored vehicles, and other relics of war left behind by Ethiopian army were dumped. Although it is place of interest but after watching the site, I was thinking what war gives us. Destruction, death, waste of money and resources are the outcome of war.

*St. Mary's Orthodox Church:*

The church was constructed in the year 1938. It is located on top of a small hill. It was built with red bricks with two huge bell towers located in front of the entrance. Inside the church there are large number of Byzantine paintings of Angeles and religious icons including that of St. Mary's. Location of the church including its inside view gives lot of pleasure in mind. One will have automatically spiritual feelings in the area itself.

Besides the above, museum, zoo, architecture of the post office, Mainefhi-dam (20 kilometers away) and cemetery are other places of interest in and around Asmara.

**Few Other Places of Tourist-Interest**

*Debre Bizen Monastery*

Soon after leaving Asmara towards east, the road passes through Hindu and the British cemeteries. These persons died in Second World War. After 20 kilometers drive from Asmara, Nefasit town comes. It is on way to Massawa (port city). In Nefasit, the monastery of Debre Bizen is located at about 2400 meters above sea level. It was constructed in the year 1361. One has to go on foot (rather climb) to reach the monastery. People normally start very early morning. Women are not allowed to visit. It is believed that Abune Filipos who constructed the monastery wanted that her monks should not be tempted to women.

### *Kohaito*

It is located 11 kilometers south of Adi-Keih the place is known for archaeological site "Queen of Sheba Dam", believed to be a place of worship. It was constructed in between 400 and 500 B.C. archaeologists believe that if site is excavated then many things would be revealed.

### *Metera*

Metera is located about 135 kilometers away of South of Asmara. It has been partially excavated. Iron cross on mount Metera and five meters Steala (obelisk) with an inscription of third century are worthy sites to be seen. Partial excavation has revealed that it was a growing city inhabited by crowded residential areas.

### *Ham-Debre Libanos*

This is a monastery constructed in the early 6th century by the Syrian missionaries. The place is about 150 kilometers away from Asmara. Originally it was located in Ham village and later on shifted to below the Ham plateau. Its church contains "Golden Gospel", a metal covered the Bible that date back to 13th century. A large number of mummified bodies were discovered here. According to some experts these mummies were 500 years old. The bodied were wrapped with cloth and animal skins.

*Semenawi Bahri*

This area is full of thick forest and animals. Animals like baboons and vervet monkeys are widely found here. According to Wild Life Department of Eritrea government leopards, kudu, push buck, warthog, duiker etc are also available. The place is also home for different types of flora and fauna. Soothing sound of birds brings peace and happiness to the visitors. It is an unimaginable situation. One can only realize and enjoy the beauty only after the visit.

## WESTERN LOW LAND OF ERITREA

The low land varies from 300 meters to 1000 meters. It is believed that original indigenous population in western Eritrea was of 8th millennium B.C. Microlithic tools reveal that it was in the "stone age." Evidence on breeding of cattle and goats during third and fourth millennium B.C. were found here. In the 2nd millennium B.C. the lands were more or less used by nomadic and semi-nomadic people. Many of them came far away to the north and west belong to Nara and Kunama communities. It is believed that both the communities have their origins long ago in the lands of the Nile.

The main arterial road through the western low lands descends from high land plateau to the west of Keren. It has passed through the major towns of Agordat and Barentu, finally reached to Sudan border. The summer season in the Western low land is from April to June, when temperature exceeds 40 Degree Celsius. During that period weather is very dry and dusty. After that rain starts and ends in September. The most appropriate time to visit the Western low land is October to March.

Some of the important places of Western Low land are presented below:

*Aghordat*

Scenic town of Aghordat located in the altitude of 615 meters from the sea level lies in between the Barka and the Gash rivers. Plenty of agricultural commodities are grown in and around Aghordat.

The ruins of railway are an interesting visiting site. The railway line from Aghordat was extended up to Massawa.

The architecture of the buildings in the area depicts Turk-Egyptian style.

*Mogolo*

It is a market place for the semi-nomadic Nara people. On every Tuesday huge market takes place where traditional Nara products like basket, saddlery etc are sold.

*Barentu*

Barentu is located in the altitude of 980 meters than the sea level. It is the heart of Kunama territory. Barentu has one main street contains many shops and stalls. In this area a beautiful mosque is located in the busy main square of the road.

*Augaro*

Augaro is located 84 kilometers away from Barentu. It is a small town having a lively market. In the center (hill side) remains of the Gold mine started by the Italians in 1932 may be seen. It is reported that presently feasibility studies are being conducted to get an idea about the viability of extracting gold deposits.

*Antore*

Antore is located 117kilometers away from Barentu. It is a village having one of rolling hills and sorghum and aristida grasslands. Since it is located near the Barks river so land is very fertile vis-à-vis it's beautiful landscape.

*Tessenei*

Before reaching to Sudan, Tessenei is the last major town of Eritrea. The main square, where the buses to and from Sudan alight, is a place of cultural melting point. Cotton is abundantly grown here. Based on cotton production a processing industry has been established. A big dam in the year 1920s was constructed which provide water to 20,000 hectares of land.

*Tocombia*

Tocombia is located at about 29 kilometers away from Barentu. It is famous for the biggest market in the region (main market day is Tuesday). The Gash river of Eritrea is life of Tocombia, although it does not flow through out the year. But the surrounding area of the Gash dominated by palm trees is beautiful. In recent years tobacco plantation along the bank of the river has been taken up. The route along the river is used through out the year by vast camel trains.

*The Barka & its wildlife:*

The Barka is one of the important rivers of Eritrea. Thick woodland on the banks of the Barka is different from the rest of Eritrea. The woods comprise Zizypus, a type of palm, and various species of acacia.

The availability of water not only facilitates agricultural development, but also provides the livelihood for a wide variety of flora and fauna. In 1930s this and other parts of Eritrea were home to substantial populations of large African mammals, and now with the independence and stability their numbers are increasing.

There is still much to see of interest to wildlife enthusiasts and ornithologists. Elephants have already returned to this neck of the woods. A preliminary survey by the Eritrean wildlife unit has also identified the following species in this region: Abyssinian hare, Pale fox, Black-backed jackal, Common jackal, African wild cat, Vervet monkey, Anubis baboon, Warthong, Soemmering's gazelle, and Bushbuck.

*The Settit and its wild life*

Settit is an important river in the Western Lowland. Surrounding of the area is famous for birds and animals. Some of the species commonly spotted inter alia, include cattle egret, great white egret, guinea fowl, rand grouse, ostrich, bee-eater, gray hornbill barbet, swift, honey-guide, yellow wag tail, marabon stork, black kite, hooded vulture, lanner falcon, spotted eagle and owl.

## ANSEBA REGION: PLACES OF INTEREST

Keren is the regional capital of Anseba region. Keren is a planned city. The places of interest are Mariam Dearit, Turko-Egyptian fort, British cemetery, Italian and old railway station. Regarding Mariam Dearit, it may be mentioned that there is a big baobab tree, having a grotto inside the tree. In the grotto there is a statue of Mother Marry. It was inaugurated on July 18, 1881. It is a very auspicious place for the people of Christian faith. Every year on 29th May celebration is held here. The people of Christian faith believe that mother Marry in the dream told that she blessed the tree. It happened on 29 May, so that day is celebrated with joy and gaiety. Many persons from different corner of Eritrea visit the shrine.

Some of the important places of Northern and Southern area of Red sea are presented below:

*Denkalia*

It is the home of Afar community. Once upon a time they were known for their ferocity. The famous British explorer Sir Wilde Thesiger observed in 1932 during his expedition to Lake Abbe as "every man wore strapped across the stomach, a formidable curved dagger known as Jile, with a sixteen-inch blade sharp on each side".

In 1867 the Swiss adventurer Werner Munzinger described the beauty of the place (Denkalia and its Red sea) as "it was a magnificent night; the full moon lighted this grand and most striking event, terrific-scenery".

The geology of Denkalia has always been a great interest to the tourists and academicians. Two of its most geological features are Denakil Alps and the Depression. The Alps are over 200 kilometers long and have peaks over 2000 meter high. On other hand, the Denakil Depression, (100 meters below the sea level) is one of the hottest places on the earth.

Its volcanic basalt rocks were deposited 15 million years ago when the continents of Africa and Asia (Arab region) were separated.

*Hirgigo*

Ruins of one of the oldest mosque of Eritrea are found here.

*Foro*

It was a trading center with the Arabian Peninsula.

*Adulis*

It was an ancient trade route from Egypt to Indian Ocean. Incense was commonly traded through the route. Vast quantities of artifacts of historical importance were found in Adulis. These include gold and silver coins, marble pottery, glasses etc. most of the ruins were constructed in black basalt. There are tombs and places, "the remains of what is possible an eighth century Christian church and an temple for worshipping of sun".

*Buri-Peninsula*

Archaeological evidence reveals that once up a time, the area was full of elephants but not a single one is found now- a- days. The main settlement on Buri is the administrative center of Gelalo. It has a charming small harbour. North of Gelalo located Inghil and Doleh villages. Both are worthy places for visit. However, most impressive sight of all is the vase salt-pan of Buri. In the sun, white flats shimmer like an oasis.

National geographic magazine described the livelihood of Afars working these pans as "wresting income from a hellhole", because of the hardships caused by the sun and wind. Another fascinating feature of Buri is the large number of traditional graves.

*Badda Lake*

Its volcanic lake is a special attraction in Eritrea. Local guides' help is required to reach the place, as the lake is located in the middle of the desert.

*Thio*

Thio is a charming fishing village. It is the biggest fishing settlement in between Assab and Massawa.

*Iddi*

Iddi is an isolated hamlet in a beautiful crescent shaped bay. A very old mosque is located here.

*Assab*

Assab is a large and modern port of Eritrea. Assab is divided into three parts. Assab Seghir (small Assab) is located on the shoreline, in the center of the town is Assab Kebir (big Assab) covering the port and third part is city center, where hotels and restaurants are located.

*Massawa*

Massawa is the capital and administrative center of Northern Red sea region. It is known as 'Pearl in the Red Sea'. Massawa was first liberated during freedom struggle. It was liberated on 10th February 1990. Next to Independence Day, liberation of Massawa (locally known as Fenkel Celebration Day) is observed as second largest festival in Eritrea (Eritrea Profile, 25 November, 2006). It is an important place of Eritrea. The ancient Greeks and Egyptians regarded it as an important trading center. Turks established control over Massawa in the 16th and 17th centuries when it became a major outlet for trade in slaves, pearls, hides and fish.

Travelers from Europe who visited Massawa in the 19th century narrated about the cosmopolitan nature of the port, as the merchants from India, Middle East, and the West used the port. Massawa Island the heart of the old Turkish settlement was joined to the Twalet Island by a causeway. The extravagant villas depict Turkish architectural style. During 1950s Massawa became a thriving city during British occupation. The city was popularly known as "the Pearl of the Red Sea".

It is believed that due to proximity to Saudi Arabia prophet Mohammed's companions "the Sahaba" took shelter in this place, to avoid their persecution. Some mosques exist in the area. The Shafi mosque for example is one of the oldest mosques of Africa. The mosque is about 100 years old.

Massawa is one of the few places of the world, where yacht cruising is available. Charter yachts are available for cruising vis-à-vis for scuba driving and other water sports. In the Red Sea area Dahlak sub-region exists which is famous for its islands. There are more than 350 islands spread over to the area of 1500 square kilometers. Since 1960, no attempts have been made by the divers to visit Dahlak reefs. It is true that depending on their depth and coral formations, different reefs are suitable for scuba divers.

The coast of Massawa is also renowned for the shipwrecks. Some of these are in between 3 meters and 4 kilometers. These wrecks are mainly of Second World War. It includes warships, frigates, and even tanks. Red sea is also well known for various types of species. The different types of common and uncommon fishes, turtles, hawksbill, and green species are available. Different types of sharks are also available but the incident of attacking swimmers is a rare incident. Life under Red sea of the Massawa east coast is really a treasure of environment as different varieties of colourful fishes and exotic corals are available in plenty.

**MASSAWA VISIT:**

Due to sudden death of foreign minister of Eritrea holidays were declared in our Institute from 29th August to 31st August 2005.The foreign minister Ali Seid Abdalla was a freedom fighter and a great visionary. The people of Eritrea respect him for his role 'in the country's military, political, and diplomatic spheres since the start of the liberation struggle until the day of his death' (Eritrea Profile, 31st August 2006). So his death was great loss for the nation. With the four days holiday in our Institute was added one more day i.e. 1st September. As mentioned earlier on 1st September armed struggle started against Ethiopia. I was also disheartened for his death as he was respected person to all of us. However in view of the holidays, I decided to visit Massawa, which is about 115 kilometers away from Asmara. Without Massawa visit (due to Red Sea) visit to Eritrea is having no meaning. On 29th August 2005 I boarded a bus for Massawa. It was about 12.30 P.M. when bus finally started for Massawa. Massawa is located in lowland, so slowly we were feeling the change of climate-cold to hot. I pulled out my sweater.

Around 1.30 P.M. our bus reached to a small town named Ghinda, which is about 50 kilometers away from Asmara. The bus stopped for about 30 minutes, I took cool drinks and some "Balas". Balas is a cactus fruit widely available during July to September. The fruit is delicious and cheap (each one fruit costs around 50 paise). The people collect from the plants and sell everywhere, mainly besides the roads. They need not require paying any money for fruit collection. The cactus plants are taller than Indian cactus, even 6-7 feet tall and spread over to wide area. In one plant 100 or even more than 100 fruits are grown. The fruit size looks like a small mango. The fruits are plucked from the trees by wearing hand gloves in order to avoid thorns. The sellers cut both sides of "balas" first and then horizontally cut the outer layer and peel out the layer. After that they serve the "balas" to consumers. The entire process is done in such a way that cutting, peeling and serving are done without touching the fruit by hand. As a result full hygiene is maintained. The fruit contains lot of small seeds, which many people swallow along with the flesh of the fruit. Our bus left at Ghinda at about 2 PM. When I reached Massawa it was about 3.30P.M. In the Massawa town there are some hotels but tourists prefer to stay in beach hotels. There are two beach hotels in Massawa. I wanted to enjoy Red Sea and its beach so I hired a taxi from bus station and reached to Hamasien hotel (about 10 kilometers away). Earlier I booked a room in the hotel so I did not face any problem for the room. After completing all the formalities I occupied an air-conditioned room. After couple of minutes spending in the room with a towel I went to beach. It is few meters away from the hotel. The water is very salty but neat and clean. I was told Red Sea was not polluted by industrial waste. In and around the beach area no shops for food, tea, snacks, handicrafts and clothes are available. Any beach in India or in Iran (Caspian Sea) contains number of shops.

Food items of limited varieties are only available in the hotels. One of the reasons is that through out the year many tourists do not visit Massawa. The temperature during summer soars up to 48 Degree Celsius. Winter is the best season to visit Massawa, but period is very limited.

Massawa and Asmara had railway network. The railway line was also established from Asmara to Keren and Agordat. All these were constructed in late 19$^{th}$ and early 20$^{th}$ centuries. During the time of war with Ethiopia, the railway lines were destroyed in 1975-76. However after independence Government has reconstructed the Asmara to Massawa rail lines. The journey is beautiful as it passes through valleys, bridges, and culverts atop riverbeds. Mention may be made here that Italians constructed ropeways from Asmara to Massawa. It was about 75 kilometers long and considered as longest ropeways in the world. During Second World War British destroyed completely the glorious ropeways and sold to other countries.

Red sea is very calm and quiet. No huge waves can be seen or roaring sound is heard. People can walk-in to the sea from the shore half kilometer without hurdles. Due to the presence of Reddish Algae, the sea looks red in color. I spent about an hour in the Red sea. Few tourists including some foreigners were also enjoying bath in the Red sea. Some of them helped me to take my snaps. Evening I spent in the hotel and after dinner again I went to the seashore. Although light was limited but my visit was immediately after full moon, so I enjoyed the beauty of the sea at night. Next day early morning again I rushed to the sea for morning bath. This time water was little cold. Many persons also took bath. Some of the tourists were putting mud on the body and thus cleaning themselves. I enjoyed Red Sea both evening and morning. After the bath again I took bath in the hotel as sea water is always salty. I took my breakfast and then proceed for Asmara. By evening I reached Asmara. This was an unforgettable moment for me as there are many seas in the world but Red Sea is somewhat different than other seas.

## VACATION IN OUR INSTITUTE: VISIT TO INDIA

We were busy with examination and evaluation in October and November 2005. During evaluation I observed some of the students were very good if they are guided properly they can come to international level. After the evaluation, Institute declared vacation for one month starting from 1st December 2005. Some of us planned to visit India to meet our families. Some of them having families so stayed back. On 2nd December 2005 in the mid night by Yemeni airlines we reached Mumbai via Sana'a, capital of Yemen. The flight first reached to Khartoum, capital of Sudan. Many passengers got down and many also boarded. In Sudan airport there were many United Nations flights. Some parts of Sudan those days were suffering from internal law and order problem. In view of this, United Nations interfered. However, in the mid-night the flight started from Khartoum and early morning at about 5A.M. (India 7:30A.M.) flight landed at Sana'a. Our next connecting flight for Mumbai was at 8 P.M. (India 10:30P.M.). Yemeni airlines arranged our stay in a hotel in Sana'a, which was in the center of the city. As a result we could see the important places including markets of Sana'a. The flight from Sana'a started at about 8P.M. first it stopped to Aden (a port city of Yemen). As usual some passengers got down and some others boarded. In the process it took about an hour. Finally, we reached Mumbai at about 4 A.M. of 4th December 2005. We were about 25 Indians from different parts of our country. I purchased an Indian airlines ticket at Mumbai airport for Hyderabad. The flight was delayed (supposed to leave

Mumbai by 9A.M.) by couple of hours. I reached Hyderabad at 1 P.M.

My return ticket to Asmara was on 5$^{th}$ January 2006, so I could spend one month with my family in India. On 5$^{th}$ January some of our friends also planned to come back to Eritrea. So in Mumbai airport we all met. Flight departed Mumbai at 6:30 P.M, without any stop at Aden. This time only after reaching Asmara flight goes to Khartoum and also no halt at Sana'a. At about 2 A.M. (Eritrea time) of 6$^{th}$ January, we reached Asmara.

## CELEBRATION OF INDIAN REPUBLIC DAY IN ERITREA

After coming from India although I was cherishing the sweet memories but my mind was little upset as for another one year I would be out of my family. This was neutralized to a great extent on Republic Day. Our army along with army of other countries is posted in Eritrea under the banner of "United Nations Mission in Ethiopia and Eritrea" (UNMEE). Last couple of years they are posted. Every six months, a new batch of army comes from the same country. They replace the old batch. Our army every year celebrates both Republic Day and Independence Day in Eritrea. They invite Indians working in Asmara. This time celebration in a foreign country that too in our army camp, which I witnessed first time in life, gave me lot of pleasure. Indian army camp is located at about 10 Kilometers away from our Institute. Institute arranged bus and we all reached there by 11A.M. The flag was hoisted by a senior army officer, Col. S.S. Saigal at 11:30 A.M. About 150 Indians many of them with their families attended. After a brief ceremony lunch was extended to all participants. It was a good experience for all of us as we could meet many Indian friends working at different places of Asmara/Eritrea. It is pertinent to mention here that about 700 Indians are working in Eritrea mostly in teaching field in various capacities.

## MY TV INTERVIEW

One of my memorable events in Eritrea was television interview in Eritrea National TV channel. Both recording and interview were held on 14th February 2006. Interview took place at about 3 P.M. and it was aired at 10 P.M. The programme was for half an hour. General type of discussions about Eritrea, such as its educational development, about our institute (EIT), etc were held. I started by greetings the people in local language and also ended with local language i.e., instead of telling Thank you, "Yekenyelai". Next few days many persons (whom I did not know even) congratulated me for the programme. In fact, before the show I was little worried as some of my very close Indian friends advised me not to discuss any controversial matters. So I was always cautious on my replies.

## MY WIFE AND SON'S VISIT TO ERITREA:

On 21st April 2006 my wife and son came to Eritrea for one month. It was a sudden visit as initially they did not plan. As per terms and conditions of appointment, wife ticket (spouse ticket) would be provided/reimbursed by the Government of Eritrea. My only son completed his 10th standard examination. My wife is a teacher. They came see to me for a month, re-union of family. In time of coming they came by Yemeni airlines along with some of my colleagues' wives. As a part of the journey one-day night halt plus full day was available in Sana'a. Yemeni airlines arranged board and lodging in a hotel without any payment. They enjoyed the place, because always in a group, enjoyment is more than single traveling. They reached here on 21st April 2006. That day onward was holiday in our Institute. The day 21st April was Good Friday followed by Easter, continuous four days holiday. Good Friday is observed about a month later than India as Eritreans follow different calendar. On 23rd April we decided to visit Massawa. Early morning we went by government bus, by afternoon we reached there. As booked earlier we stayed in a beach hotel. Immediately after reaching all of us went to have bath in the Red sea. My son thoroughly enjoyed. We spent more than an hour in the sea. This time I enjoyed more as earlier I was alone now with family so different environment. Photographs were taken with some foreign tourists. Next day afternoon, we came back to Asmara.

After coming from Asmara, next week we planned to visit another beautiful city of Eritrea, Keren. There is a saying that without seeing Keren, visit to Eritrea is not complete. Keren visit was organized by a Government department namely Savings and Micro- credit Department (SMCP). This Department helps poor people by extending credit through self-help groups. I did some studies in India about self-help groups. So after coming to Eritrea, I contacted SMCP and they showed me some schemes in Asmara region and Debub region. Based on this I published articles in local newspaper and Indian journals. It may be mentioned here that in November 2005, SMCP officials took me to a village namely Maiduma, located in Ethiopia border to show some of their beneficiaries. Maiduma is located at about 115 kilometers away from Asmara. Initially about 60 kilometers road is good, rest is fair weather (in Indian word *Kutcha*). Ethiopian army raged this village in May 2000. People badly suffered, but through Government effort vis-à-vis by the efforts of SMCP many poor persons could change their economic condition. It was a good experience for me. Based on this study, I published an article also. As a part of the further study, Keren visit was planned. It was about 7.30 AM of 29 April, three of us (wife, son and self) started along with one officer of SMCP to Keren by SMCP's vehicle. Keren is 90 kilometers away from Asmara, capital of Anseba province/zoba. Our destination is further 25 kilometers away from Keren, Hagaz village. We reached at about 10 AM at Hagaz village. By this time many beneficiaries of SMCP gathered near a school. They all belong to Bilein community. The beneficiaries include both Muslims and Christians. I collected information from them. There is a research methodology called Participatory Rural Appraisal (PRA). I used this for my study. After completing the study we came to Keren city where I interviewed some more beneficiaries. With the completion of the study we went to see places of Keren city. Keren is a beautiful city. Buildings and roads are well planned. European touch is observed everywhere. The officer of SMCP offered us good lunch in a restaurant. After the lunch we went to see 'Mother Mariam Tree' locally known as 'Mariam Da'arit'. This is a big baobab tree, having a grotto in inside the tree. In the grotto, there is a statue of Mother Marry. It was inaugurated on July 18, 1881. As mentioned earlier the people of Christian faith believe that mother Marry in the dream told that she blessed the tree. It happened on 29 May, so that day is celebrated with joy and gaiety. Many persons from different corner of Eritrea visit the shrine. Otherwise also everyday people visit the area. In the grotto people light candle and donate money in the donation box. The surroundings of the tree and its area are beautiful and neatly maintained. It is spread over to an area of 10 hectares with tress like neem, orange etc. We all prayed to Mother and sought her blessing.

My wife and son left for India on 17$^{th}$ May 2006.

## VISIT TO INDIAN ARMY CAMP

As an Indian I am proud of many respects. One is about our army. In many books and literature from childhood I read our army is the most discipline army in the world. May be for this reason in any United Nations Peace Keeping Mission, there is great demand for our army.

I also observed many Eritreans have high regards for our army.

Once I visited our army camp on Republic Day. This time I had to visit for my ailment. In our Institute a volleyball match was organized among the teaching staff on 28th September 2006. I was one of the players. During the course of play due to dust, my right eye got infected. Couple of days I suffered badly, consulted a doctor also. Even then I did not get rid of the problem. Some of my friends suggested consulting our army doctors. I visited the army camp on 3rd October afternoon. By this time new contingent has come. After six months old contingent is replaced by new contingent. During the time of my visit Medical Officer was not available. The Para-medical staff after examining me gave some medicines - eye drops and tablets at free of cost. They offered me tea also. Within four days I was cured. When I was suffering I was very much worried as I myself was cooking food and taking classes for which eyes should be okay. So after get rid of the problem, I conveyed my grateful thanks to them. Their hospitality, sober behaviour and attitude, I will always remember. Our strength is our unity. Many foreigners in Eritrea (mainly Europeans) told me, "Your country is incredible". There is no doubt about the statement.

## ASSOCIATION WITH PAKISTANI COLLEAGUES

In the year 2006, 15 persons from Pakistan joined in our Institute. Due to some problems 4 of them left. Finally 11 persons stayed. Even in our batch (2005), some Indian friends after coming went back due to health and personal problem. In a foreign country everything cannot be expected like our homeland. However with the Pakistanis we have cordial relation. One of them joined in our department also. Many of them spontaneously congratulated me for my publications, when published in the only English newspaper of Eritrea. With the request of my department colleague, we together published an article also. I have observed all of them want good relation with us (India). I pray Mata Kamakhya that those days should not be very far, when we will have good relation between two brotherly neighbours - no death, no destruction and no madness.

## RETURN TO INDIA

As mentioned earlier my term in Eritrea was for two years, so I have to return and join in my Institute in India. Although many academicians of Eritrea requested me to continue for another two years but I expressed my helplessness in this regard. Along with me 21 colleagues who joined at the same time also decided to return for good. Since I would come back, many of my Indian, Eritrean and Pakistani friends invited me for dinner. I would like to mention the event of 31st December. On 31st December I had dinner invitation by my colleague and friend Dr. Sadasivuni Krishna Rao, Head-Department of Anthropology, Sociology and Political Science in an Arabic hotel. It was eve of New Year 2007. Roads were full of people, many shops mainly bar and restaurants were open up to mid night. People bid farewell to 2006 and welcome 2007 by bursting of crackers and blowing horn of vehicles. We all enjoyed. Although I had many invitations before my return to India but I mentioned this to explain the event of 31st December evening.

Finally on 14th January, early morning we left Eritrea for good via Dubai. Our plane was via Djibouti a small country of Africa. It's capital is also Djibouti. The flight halted here for about three hours, albeit halting schedule was an hour. Due to some technical problems, it was delayed. We had a glance of Djibouti. Hardly any multi-storied building can be seen in the capital.

Finally we reached at mid-day in Dubai. Another time I had an opportunity to see Dubai, where earlier I visited on way to Iran. On 15th January 2007 reached at Hyderabad and re-united with family.

## REFERENCES

Eritrea: Come, fall in Love, (2005), Ministry of Tourism, the State of Eritrea.

Eritrea Profile, (Only English News paper of Eritrea) June 22, 2005.

Eritrea Profile, August 31, 2005.

Eritrea Profile, May 13, 2006.

Eritrea Profile, October 25, 2006.

Eritrea Profile, 25 November 2006.

Eritrea: A Country Handbook, Ministry of Information, 2002.

**A view of Asmara City**

**Author with Indian friends in a hotel in Asmara**

**Eritreans Playing Local Musical Instrument**

**Selling of Cactus Fruits**

**Front View of Cathedral**

**A Happy Evritrea Family**

**A View of Asmara City**

**Red Sea**

**Cactus Plant**

**A Market Place in Asmara**

**State of Mother Mariam in Keren**

**A Monument in Maiduma near Ethiopia Border**

# Annexure-1

## Food for all: Implementation of Telefood Project (A project of Food and Agriculture Organisation in Iran)

### ABOUT TELEFOOD

Food is the basis need for survivability of human being, in that matter for any creature. Even then many people in the world are not having sufficient food every day to fulfill their stomach. The Food and Agriculture Organisation (FAO) statistics show around 800 million people go hungry everyday because they don't have access to food to feed themselves and their families. In view of this Tele Food Project has been taken up by FAO in 1997 in various countries of the world including India. The objective of Tele Food is to help and ensure that all people have the access to food i.e., Food for All. This is done through the development of various projects funded by FAO. More than 700 micro projects are presently going on in various countries, which have been financed by FAO under Tele Food Fund. Farm families in Cambodia, beekeepers in Samoa, small-scale farmers in Honduras, watermelon growers in china and fish sellers in Burkina Faso are some of the examples that have been benefited under Tele Food Project. It is heartening to note that women are the major beneficiaries of Tele Food Projects. Around half of the micro projects funded under Tele food are meant for women. The fund is raised mainly by donations. Over 6 million US $ has been raised since Tele Food began in 1997.

Every paise collected through the Tele food purpose is used to finance small grass root projects costing less than US 10,000$

each. No money is diverted for administrative costs, experts, training or meetings, that is, for unproductive purpose. One such scheme sponsored under Tele Food Project in Iran is discussed here.

Iran is divided into 28 provinces, 252 townships and 680 districts. Each province is administered by a Governor-General, each township by a Governor and each district by Lieutenant Governor. Khorasan province is the largest province of Iran with 313000 sq. kms area.

Some other basic features of Iran are presented in Table 1.

**Table 1**

**Some other basic features of Iran**

| | |
|---|---|
| 1. Total area of Iran | 1648000sq. kms. |
| 2. Total population (1996 Census) | 60 million |
| (a) Urban population | 37 million |
| (b) Rural population | 23 million |
| 3. Total employed population | 14.5 million |
| (a) Employment in agriculture | 23.04 per cent |
| (b) Employment in Industry | 30.7 per cent |
| (c) Employment in service sector | 44.5 per cent |
| 4. Literacy rate (6 years & above) | 79.51 per cent |
| (a) Literacy among male | 84.66 per cent |
| (b) Literacy among female | 74.21 per cent |
| 5. Agricultural land out of total land area of Iran | 11.00 per cent |

*Source:* Iran at a Glance, 1998, Iran, Tehran

## STUDY AREA

The study has been carried out at Shahidabad village in Mazandaran province of Iran in the month of May 2001.

## ABOUT MAZANDARAN PROVINCE

The province Mazandaran is one of 28 provinces of Iran. Its capital, Sari, is situated at about 250 kms, away from Tehran.

Mazandaran is spread over to 24091 square kilometers. consisting 1.5 per cent are of the country. As per 1996 census, total population was 2.6 million in the province against 60 million in Iran. The share of rural and urban population is 54 per cent and 4 per cent respectively. 60 per cent of its area is under forest.

The province is considered as rice basket of Iran as 42 per cent of total rice production of Iran comes from the province. Different types of Citrus fruits are widely grown in the area. Out of total horticultural production, 10 per cent is produced in the province. Kiwi is the important horticultural crop in the province. Meat - chicken and red meat – is also widely available in the area. The annual average production of chicken and red meat is 80,000 tones and 50, 000 tones respectively.

The Tele Food Project has been taken up at Shahidababad village of Mazandaran. The earlier name of the village was Terujen but later on its name has been changed to Shahidabad. The word Shahidabad has been derived from, the Farsi word "Shahid" meaning martyr. During the time for was with Iraq (in 1980s) many soldiers hailing from the village were killed, so the name has been changed to Shahidabad. It may be mentioned here that the graves of the soldiers are maintained by the villagers in the heart of the village. In front of each grave, a box has been constructed where the photograph along with name of the soldier have been depicted. The graves are maintained and respected by the villagers themselves. Every morning they keep some flowers on the graves, which greatly impressed me. Because this is an indication of patriotism as even after 14 years of completion of war they regularly pay homage.

## ABOUT TELE FOOD PROJECT

There are more than 700 households in the village. Almost all the households are having some piece of agricultural land where crops like wheat, paddy, cotton and sunflower along with fruits are grown. The land holding varies greatly, much below 10 hectares to more than 30 hectares. The villagers reported that due to lack of irrigation, productivity is low as well as cropping intensity. Almost all the households are having 20-30 chickens. They consume lot of protein in the form of red meat and chicken.

In the year 2000, (October) 5 poor women headed-families of Shahidabad were assisted under Tele food project of FAO. They were provided with poultry bind (chicken) scheme. As part of the scheme building for the chicks, chicks feed, container etc., were included. A women member of the group voluntarily donated a piece of land for construction of poultry shed. Total schematic cost was around $1500 US (1$=8,000 Rials. Rial is their currency), out of which $1247 was provided under Tele food project and balance amount was arranged by the Ministry of Jihad and Agriculture, Government of Iran. Again out of $1247, an amount of $ 538 was spent for construction of poultry shed (cement flooring with cement wall and asbestos roof), an amount of $ 82 was spent to construct a godown for storing feed, $155 was meant for equipments like water vessels, feed containers, cool box etc., and $472 was spent for purchase of chicks, feed, vaccination of chicken etc. The chicks for 1-day old are purchased and normally after 37 days, i.e., 37-38 days old chicks are sold. Each chicken fetched 0.66$.

The building of the scheme was constructed under the supervision of officials of district Jihad and Agriculture. They also arranged training of women members about rearing and vaccination of poultry birds for which entire cost was borne by Jihad office. Vaccination is very important component of the scheme otherwise diseases may totally ruin. It is reported that the chickens in the area suffer from diseases like New castle, chicken pox and Pasteurellosis for which time to time vaccination is done. The district Jihad ad Agriculture Office also monitors each and every aspect of the project including backward and forward linkages.

At the time of visit, all the five women in presence of many other villagers informed that in three occasions chickens were sold. Each of the members was paid $20 US and balance amount was invested to purchase chick etc. The village is situated near the town Behshar as a sequel marketing of chicken is not the problem, rather chicken have great demand in the area.

The money as well as account is maintained by a group leader but not kept in the bank. Since the scheme is in initial stage so the beneficiaries we more interested to expand it. It was observed that other villagers about the scheme. During the course of discussion, beneficiaries informed that they would like to have one additional room for staying and watching so the no one can take away chickens, as the building is located slightly at a isolated place so the possibility of theft is not ruled out. Except this, otherwise they have no major problem or grievance. It was observed that the scheme has brought ray of hope to five poor families as many of them earn their livelihood by working as agricultural labourers and two of the women are widows also. Their view is that self-employment gives self-respect and moreover they can prove their entrepreneurial skill, which is otherwise not possible in wage labour.

## CONCLUSION

In this paper an attempt has been made to highlight the Tele Food Project of FAO. It is meant for the poor people to earn through income generation activities. It was observed in the village that many other women were also interested in this type of scheme. It acted as a 'Demonstration Effect'.

*Source:* Indian Economic Panorama, NewDelhi, January 2002

# Annexure-2

## Poverty in Eritrea: Some Observations and Suggestions

Poverty is still a major problem in the world as number of poor people is still huge in the world. In the countries like Niger, people are badly suffering due to poverty. Calorie value of food is normally base to calculate poverty. It is believed that an adult person requires minimum 2200-2300 calorie of food value per day. Based on this, income is calculated. Any person or family is having less than minimum income, the person/family is considered living Below the Poverty Line (BPL). Economists believe that impact of growth-oriented development did not trickle down to the poor. In view of this, many countries have initiated poverty alleviation programs from time to time, which showed positive result.

The case of India may be referred in this context. Poverty ratio was very high in India, during 1973-74 as out of total population 54.9 percent population was living Below the Poverty Line (BPL). The poverty ratio in rural and urban areas was 56.4 percent and 49.0 percent respectively during the same period. Considering the seriousness of the problem the Government of India initiated several steps to eradicate poverty from the country. These inter alia, include launching of self-employment and wage-employment programs, construction of houses at free of cost etc. As a result, poverty ratio declined to 36 percent by 1993-94 further to 26 percent in recent years.

The State of Eritrea is also serious to alleviate poverty from the country. As a preliminary step, National Statistics & Evaluation Office (NSEO) conducted "Household Living

Standard Measurement Survey" in 2003 with a view to get thorough idea about the nature, extent and causes of poverty. In the meantime, three other studies on poverty were also completed in Eritrea. These are Participatory Poverty Assessment study, second study is on Second Demographic & Health Survey and third one is the Rural Livelihood Security Assessment study. Based on these, NSEO produced a Report under the title of "Dimensions of Poverty in Eritrea". The poverty data reveal that overall poverty ratio in the country is 66.40 percent with rural and urban percentages are 64.64 and 70.32 respectively. The Report also mentioned about "Extreme Poor" category. In Eritrea also like other countries poverty (BPL) is calculated on the basis of money value. Accordingly, 240 Nakfa per capita per month is the BPL line and 150 Nakfa per capita per month is for extreme poor. That is any one earning less than 240/150 Nakfa per month will come in the category of poor/extreme poor. The data on poverty are depicted in the following table.

**Incidence of Poverty (Head Count) in Eritrea**

| *Rural / Urban* | *% of Poor* | *% of Extreme Poor (Out of Total Poor)* |
|---|---|---|
| Rural | 64.64 | 38.90 |
| Urban | 70.32 | 32.65 |
| Total | 66.40 | 36.97 |

As mentioned already the State of Eritrea is sincere to alleviate poverty from the country. However few suggestions are extended by the author for poverty alleviation from the country.

- Self-employment and wage-employment programs may be initiated for enhancing income of the poor. One of the strategies for implementation of self-employment program is formation of self-help groups (SHGs). After successful experiment of SHGs in Bangladesh by Md.

Yunus, many countries have adopted the approach. On the other hand, wage employment program can be implemented through creation of infrastructure, which will generate employment vis-à-vis community assets will also be created.

- Agriculture, fishery and animal husbandry are the important activities of the people of Eritrea as 80 percent of its people depend on these. But contribution of these sectors to Gross Domestic Product (GDP) is around 20 percent. The reasons inter alia, include shortage of skilled manpower, low investment etc. So with the increase in investment of agriculture and animal husbandry not only income of the poor will increase, share of GDP will also rise. It is also suggested that there is potential to develop agriculture in the country by extending more areas under cultivation. As out of total potential area of 2.1 million hectare of arable land, about 500,000 hectare is under cultivation at present. Once more areas are brought under agriculture vis-à-vis investment in agriculture increases, employment opportunities will increase, purchasing power of the people will increase, and hence aggregate demand will rise. Thus there will be "Multiplier Effect" in the economy.

Animal husbandry is another potential area, which is having enormous scope for development as it contributes in export also, besides meeting local demand. For example, in the year 1992 altogether 1525 live animals were exported from Eritrea which went up to 4625 in 2003 vis-à-vis export of hides and skins also increased substantially in recent years.

*Source:* Eritrea Profile, 28 September 2005

# Annexure-3

## Development of Education in Eritrea in Post-liberation Period: Some Observations

In the modern world human resource development gets top priority in all the countries, particularly in the developing countries, as no nation can develop if human resource is neglected. For the development of human resource, basic education is sine qua non for the children. It is envisaged that government of any country plays pivotal role to impart education to its masses. Eritrea is one of the countries where government has taken several steps for the development of education after its liberation. As a result new schools and academic institutions have come up in the country. A few of the academic institutions inter alia, include College of Nursing and Health Technology, Orotta Medical School, E.I.T Mai Nefhi, etc. Many more other institutions are also coming up in the country. However, for the development of education for the common people steps are required at the grass root level that is, from the elementary level onwards. If all the children get proper education then nation will develop in true sense. In Eritrea the impact of education can be observed after liberation through its declining illiteracy rate. As per the World Bank publication (Source -The Little Data Book, 2001, World Bank) in 1990, illiteracy among male was 42 percent (15 years and above), which declined substantially in 1999 with 33 percent. The illiteracy among female was 72 percent (15 years and above), which came down to 61 percent in 1999. The World Bank statistics clearly reveal that education development programs initiated by the Government of Eritrea in the post liberation period have yielded benefit for the common people. In this context, a few statistics collected from "Eritrea: Basic Education Statistics", 2001 -02, Ministry of Education are analyzed.

## ENROLMENT OF STUDENTS

In the last year of pre-liberation that is in 1990-91, total enrolment of students in all the grades (elementary, middle and secondary) were 168783 which increased to about three times by 2001-02 within an absolute number of 481343. Within a span of 10-11 years around three-fold increase in enrolment is a matter of great achievement. Heartening to mention here that enrolment in government schools during the same period has gone up from 76 percent to 93 percent.

## ENROLMENT OF FEMALE STUDENTS

Social scientists believe that no nation can develop if fruits of development do not reach to the girls /female. As a primary step imparting education to women is sine qua non as "educated mother means educated children". The Basic Education Statistics data show that total female enrolment was 82062 in 1990-91, which went up to 205939 in 2001-02 with more than two - fold increase.

## ENGAGEMENT OF TEACHERS

Teachers are considered as the main instrument for developing of the society. With out qualified teachers students cannot be imparted quality education. So government's role in this regard is well accepted. During 1990-91, out of 4504 teachers, government teachers were 3437 (76.3%) in Eritrea. Within a span of 10-11years the number of teachers increased to 10446 and share of government teachers increased around 90 percent as their number shot up to 9377 by 2001-02. From 1990-91 to 2001-02, strength of female teachers was also enhanced, as their number was double than the earlier number.

## SCHOOL OWNERSHIP

The number of school under government has increased several folds in post liberation period. The number of government elementary school was 137 in 1990-91 which increased by more than 4 times (610) in 2001-02. Against this back -drop non-government school increased marginally i.e. 77 to 85. The data on middle school reveal high increase of government middle school in post liberation period. In the year 1990-91, number of such government school was 37, which went up to 130 in 2001-02. On the other hand there was no increase in non-government school during the same period, as their number remained same with 22. In case of secondary school, the number of government school went up to 38 in 2001-02 against 16 in 1990-91. The marginal increase (3 to 6) in non-government school was observed during this period. With respect to technical education, the data show tremendous growth of such institutions in post liberation period, as there was only one government technical institution in 1990-91, which went up to 7 in 2001-02.In case of non-government technical education before liberation there was no such institution but after liberation the number went up to 3 in 2001-02.

## CONCLUSION

The above analysis has been carried out to highlight the initiatives taken by the Government of Eritrea for the development of education after its liberation. The steps taken in this regard are really laudable as in all the above-mentioned areas several folds increase are observed. However before winding up, it is suggested that to encourage students for attending the schools (particularly for the poor segments of the society), Government may introduce free-food scheme from elementary school onwards. Such type of scheme popularly known, as "Mid-day Meal Scheme" has been proved successful in India as dropout rate has been drastically reduced in India. The Government of Eritrea may consider introducing such type of scheme in Eritrea also.

(Source: Eritrea Profile, 23 July 2005)

# Annexure-4

## Women in Eritrea Moving Towards Progress: Some Observations

Fruits of development should be reached to all sections of the people particularly to the women. Social scientists believe that without the development of women no development in real sense can take place. World Bank in its World Development Report, 1993, clearly stated that mothers' levels of health and education are closely related to children's survival and quality of life. Employment for women is also an issue. It is believed (through various studies) that "unemployment for women implies not only a deterioration in their living standards but also an increase in their dependence on husband or family; a loss of autonomy as well as security". Moreover, various studies have revealed that if women members earn in that case entire earning is spent on welfare of the family members particularly for the children. So education and employment are the two issues, which have been analyzed here in the context of women of Eritrea. One thing is clear that if need arises women of Eritrea are capable to tackle the problems. Of the total households of Eritrea, 30 per cent (approx.) of the households are headed by women (of whom 18 per cent are widows)...... "the legacy of long war of independence".

### EDUCATION

Education is an important indicator of development. Without human resource development no development in true sense can take place. In Eritrea education has been getting importance after its independence. Setting up of Eritrea Institute of

Technology (EIT, Mai Nefhi), Agriculture College at Keren, Marine College at Massawa are some of the laudable steps in this regard. However, education means "education at elementary stage". In this context, a few of the findings focusing on female / women education collected from recent publication of "Eritrea: Essential Education Indicators, 2002/03", Ministry of Education, Eritrea may be referred.

## ENROLMENT RATIO

At the elementary level, net enrolment ratios of male and female students were 24.37 per cent and 25.29 per cent respectively in 1991-92, which have increased 53.37 per cent (male) and 46.77 per cent (female) in 2002-03. The data on middle level education show net enrolment ratios of male and female were 9.08 per cent and 9.10 per cent respectively during 1991-92 which have gone up to 18.90 and 13.60 per cents respectively in 2002-03.

## FEMALE TEACHERS

It is evident from the report that in 1991-92, out of total teachers the percentage of female teachers was 8.8 and the percentage shot up to 11.0 in 2002-03. It means more and more women are not only getting higher education but also joining in the teaching profession of higher level.

## EMPLOYMENT SCENARIO

Employment is broadly categorized into two- self-employment and wage-employment. In Eritrea, 30 per cent women are in the labour force. This is really an important indicator of women's development. In other words, it can be said that many of the women (30% of labour fore) would not like to be confined in four-walls of the house. They are as dynamic as men.

## SELF-EMPLOYMENT

The study conducted by National Statistics and Evaluation Office (NSEO) of Eritrea reveal that 66 per cent of total population live below the poverty line. As is known to all,

Government of Eritrea has been sincerely trying to eradicate poverty from the country. The Savings and Micro Credit Program (popularly known as SMCP) is the largest (government-owned program) in terms of both membership and amount of outstanding loans. SMCP's credit is available to the borrowers under first tier and second tier. First-tier basically consists of beneficiaries (clients in SMCP's language) of Self-Help Groups and Second-Tier beneficiaries are individual. It is heartening to note that more and more women were the clients of SMCP. The authors studied many beneficiaries at the Himbirti village and Mai-duma village, where it was observed that women (particularly poor women) have proved successful entrepreneurs by utilizing SMCP's credit. Percentage of women availing SMCP's credit may be seen from the following table.

**Percentage of Women beneficiaries (clients) covered under SMCP credit**

| | *Percentage of Women beneficiaries* | |
|---|---|---|
| Year | I-Tier | II-Tier |
| 1996 | 30.00 | - |
| 1997 | 30.26 | 14.29 |
| 1998 | 27.62 | 6.45 |
| 1999 | 29.60 | 14.29 |
| 2000 | 30.18 | 29.00 |
| 2001 | 37.00 | 36.00 |
| 2002 | 40.00 | 36.00 |
| 2003 | 40.00 | 39.00 |
| 2004 | 42.60 | 42.04 |

*Source:* SMCP 2004 Annual Report, March 2005.

It is evident from the table that more and more women are the beneficiaries of SMCP's credit, except 1998 and 1999, which were the years affected by war.

## WAGE-EMPLOYMENT

In case of wage-employment Medium & Large Scale Manufacturing Establishments (MLSMEs) may be referred. These are major source of employment. In these establishments percentage of women employed is really encouraging, as 46.3 per cent of Eritrean women are employed against 52.2 per cent male persons. (A small percentage of non-Eritrean Male and female workers were also there).In absolute terms, 6857 women were employed in 2004, where as in 2003 & 2004, the number employed women was 6486 & 6243 respectively.

## CONCLUSION

It is evident from the above that Eritrean women have been participating in the development process whether it is in education, self-employment or wage-employment. Before winding up the case of "Lijjat Papad" from India may be mentioned here. "Papad" is a processed food made of lentil, which can be kept for longer time (1-2 years). It can be eaten after baking or fried, a popular food among the Indians. A few poor women started Papad making business under the banner of "Lijjat Papad". Now "Lijjat Papad" is a great name in India and all the poor women who started the business in a small scale now big shots. So women are capable in all respects.

(*Source:* Eritrea Profile, 26 April 2006)

# Annexure-5

## Good Bye to Poverty: Micro-credit Shows the Way

Importance of micro-credit has been realized after the successful experiment of Bangladesh Grameen Bank in early 70's. Prof. Md. Yunus of Bangladesh, a country located in South East Asia has proved that poor persons (both women & men) are having entrepreneurial skills if they are provided minimum credit to carry out the activities. His experiment is based on self-help group (SHG) approach. According to him individually a poor person may not carry out business buy if they organized in a group they are successful entrepreneurs. As we know hand consists of five fingers and all the fingers are important for hand. Same is the case of self-help group.

In Eritrea, after its independence Government took all round steps to develop the country. The biggest challenge was to eradicate poverty from the country as latest estimate shows that 66 percent of total population of Eritrea is living below that poverty line. For eradication of poverty in 1996 Savings & Micro Credit Program, (a government department) popularly known as SMCP was established.

SMCP extends credit among the poor persons who are having entrepreneurial skills. The credit is delivered in two categories. One is called First tier & other one is known as Second tier. The beneficiaries of First tier (client in SMCP's language) mainly get loan after forming self-help groups where as Second tier beneficiaries are given loan individually. Under First tier albeit beneficiaries get loan under self-help groups, but loan is meant for individual category. Here one important condition is there if all the members repay loan then the group members will get second cycle of loan. Thus under First tier beneficiaries can get loan up to ten cycles. Every time loan is made almost double. On the other hand the beneficiaries of Second tier get loan individually & it is their individual responsibility to repay loan. If they repay first cycle of loan then they are sanctioned second cycle of loan. Thus Second tier beneficiaries may get loan up to six cycles.

The performances of SMCP in terms of number of beneficiaries & in monetary terms are laudable. In the year 1996, total loan disbursed under First tier was 1370600.00 Nakfa, which was, increased 60734605.00 Nakfa in 2005. Although under Second tier no beneficiary was extended loan in 1996, but in 1997 the amount was 66755.00 Nakfa, which went up to 43069431.00 Nakfa in 2005. With respect to beneficiaries the data shows that in the year 1996, First tier beneficiaries were 1525, which went up to 20225 in 2005. Under Second tier in 1997 the number of beneficiaries was only 7 in 1997 which increased to 2284 in 2005. Within a span of 10 years such achievements of SMCP are really a noteworthy point.

To get an idea about the impact of SMCP's credit among the poor persons, an in depth study was conducted in Hagaz village of Anseba region in the last week of April 2006. A few of the beneficiaries were randomly selected & studied. All were happy to inform that micro-credit has changed their economic plight. They could reap full benefit from micro-credit. A detailed case about the impact of micro-credit is presented here.

Mohammed Ali (50 years), a farmer by occupation is having only 2 hectares of agricultural land. He was finding difficulty to derive full benefit from his land in the absence of capital. In the year 1997, he came to know about SMCP's credit. As a First tier beneficiary Mr. Ali & two of his friends formed self-help group. Each was sanctioned 750 Nakfa in 1997 as first cycle loan. Mr. Ali fully utilized & same is the case with his two other friends. He was sanctioned second cycle of loan amounting to 1500 Nakfa in 1998 (other two members also got). After repaying of loan again third cycle was sanctioned at the amount of 3000 Nakfa each in 2003. Fourth cycle of loan was sanctioned in 2004 (5000 Nakfa each). During the course of study Mr. Ali informed that he applied for 7000 Nakfa of loan as fifth cycle (other 2 members also). The amount may be released at any moment. To a query about not having loan in between 1999 & 2002, it was reported that due to war the system was disturbed. However Mr. Ali informed that he & his two other members were planning to utilize ten cycles of loan.

Mr. Ali utilized every cycle of loan by purchasing high yielding of seeds, fertilizers etc. The crops which are commonly grown by him inter alia, include millet, sorghum etc. According to him micro-credit has changed his life. He had to ask loan from his friends & relatives before the credit.. Now he is self-sufficient. In the theory of Rostow's stages of growth, Mr. Ali is in the stage of "self-sustaining growth". Although he is having ten members family (self, wife & 8 children) but basic needs are full filled.

Like Mr. Ali, others such as Mrs. Amna, Mr. Mehreteab, Mr. Keshi Malake & many others have been benefited through micro-credit. In the words of Prof. Yunus micro-credit in future will eradicate poverty from this world. According to him, " Poverty can be seen only in museum in near future".

(*Source:* Eritrea Profile, 30 August 2006)

# Annexure-6

## 'Credit' to Micro-credit: A Unique Case from Anseba Region

Poverty is a great problem in this world particularly in the developing countries. The Report of the United Nations Conference on Trade and Development (UNCTAD) on Least Developing Countries (50 Least Developing Countries in the world of which 34 are in Africa) reveals that number of people in these countries living on 1$ a day or less may go up in 2015 by 471 million against 335 million in 2000. This is a shuddering picture as instead of declining the number of poor it is expected to go up. The world leaders are concerned with the problem as it is reflected through the G8 summit, which was held in 2005 at Scotland. The leaders were under unprecedented pressure from different fronts including some of world's famous musicians to 'make poverty history', particularly in Africa. Musicians like Bono, Paul McCartney, Dido, Bjork and Chris Martin lend their voices for African cause. With this issue now another issue for discussion is about 'poverty trap'. With the increase in aid to Africa, many countries can be freed from 'poverty trap', according to Dr Jeffrey Sachs, leader of the UN Millennium Project. So it is evident that everyone is worried about poverty in the world.

The State of Eritrea is also concerned about poverty. Immediately after its independence a government department namely, Savings and Micro-credit Program, (SMCP) has been established in 1996. Micro-credit is now a popular means to eradicate poverty from the world. Prof Md.Yunus of Bangladesh through his Bangladesh Gramen Bank has already proved this.

Millions of poor people of Bangladesh, many of them women, could improve their standard of living through micro-credit. This has acted as "Demonstration Effect" in other countries of the world. For Prof. Md. Yunus relentless effort to eradicate poverty, he has been awarded noble prize this year. The Nobel Committee in its citation mentioned, "Every single individual on earth has both potential and the right to live a decent live. Across the culture and civilizations, Yunus and Gramen Bank have shown that even the poorest of the poor can work to bring about their own development".

SMCP in Eritrea has been extending credit to thousands of poor people in this country for setting up of self-employment ventures. SMCP's network has been extended after its establishment in 1996. In the year 1996, SMCP's network was confined to 4 regions and 22 sub-regions of Eritrea. Within a span of 10 years i.e. from 1996 to 2005 SMCP's network have been extended all the regions vis-à-vis 50 sub-regions. During this period, its staff strength has gone up 11 to 157. Total loan disbursement during this period has increased several folds – 1370600.00Nakfa (1996) to 103804035.88 Nakfa (2005). Altogether 22509 poor persons were benefited in 2005 against a meager number of 1525 in 1996. Different regions of Eritrea have been doing well in this regard. Achievement of Anseba region evinces that the region is faring well. Within a span of one year i.e. from 2004 to 2005 disbursement of loan in the region has increased by 99 percent. In absolute term it was 6460700.00 Nakfa in 2004 which up to almost double in 2005 with 1219600.00 Nakfa. Number of beneficiaries (client according to SMCP) has increased to 3839 in 2005 against 2697 in 2004 with 42 percent increase in relative terms. Arrear during one-year period has decreased by 18.86 percent. With these basic particulars it is evident that performance of Anseba region is laudable.

To get an idea about the impact of SMCP's credit among the poor persons, recently author visited Anseba region. A large number of beneficiaries of Hagaz and Keren were randomly contacted and necessary particulars were collected through semi-structured schedule. A unique case of a beneficiary is presented here. The case may be a micro one. But "Little drops of water, little grains of sand makes a mighty ocean and a pleasant land".

## A UNIQUE CASE FROM ANSEBA REGION:

Like many other poor persons, Debesay Goitam was one such person before getting micro-credit from SMCP. He hails from Hagaz village. A farmer by profession he is having 3 hectares of agricultural land. With 11 members family (9 children and couples) and uncertainty of rainfall (for agriculture), he was struggling for maintenance of the family at one stage. Moreover due to an accident he lost his right hand. In spite of all these, he was never disheartened and lost his hope. Rather he had zeal to establish himself as successful farmer. Up to 1995, he was somehow managing his family by cultivation of single crop in rainy season. From 1996, with the establishment of SMCP his fate was also changed. SMCP extended him credit of paltry amount of 750 Nakfa for agriculture. He utilized each and every cent of the money for agriculture without thinking of personal consumption. With the reaping of benefit, he repaid the amount within the stipulated time. In the meantime as we know normal environment was disturbed in Eritrea due to war. So again 'sun' of his fate was covered by 'cloud'. However there is a saying, "God sees the truth but waits". For Debesay the 'cloud' was dispersed in 2001 as he was sanctioned a sum of 10,000 Nakfa for his dynamism and enterprising attitude. This helped him to develop his agriculture like anything. He fully devoted himself in agriculture and repaid the loan within the stipulated period. Subsequently, he was sanctioned different cycles of loan from time to time – 20,000 Nakfa (2002), 36,000 Nakfa (2003), 40,000 Nakfa (2004) and 80,000 Nakfa (2005). He fully utilized all the loans by purchasing capital goods such as pump set with pipeline, digging of a well etc. As a variable cost, he spent to purchase seeds, fertilizers etc. Now his agriculture is not depended on nature. To a query about his growing of crop and earning of income, he reveled that he grows mainly onion for seed purpose as onion seed is having huge demand in the vicinity of the area. In fact it was observed that he has selected the activity based on 'Backward and Forward Linkages'. With regard to his net earning, within a couple of moments he informed that same hovers around 80,000 Nakfa. According to him presently eating of 'bread' and 'cake' is not a problem for him and his family members. Thanks to Prof. Md. Yunus and his Gramen Bank for introduction of the concept of micro-credit. And thanks to SMCP in Eritrea.

After the discussion, in presence of many villagers and beneficiaries of micro-credit, I wished them by telling, "Yakene Ellai". Immediately they responded "Ganjapka". I boarded in the vehicle and uttered smilingly, "Bey Salam Yaha Rakhebena". Vehicle started moving; I could hear all were uttering "Amin, Amin".

(*Source:* Eritrea Profile, 8 November 2006)

# Annexure-7

## People's Participation in Rural Development Projects: Some Observations

Development activities taken up for the people in general and rural people in particular in the present days envisage participation of the people. The term commonly used in this regard is "Beneficiary Participation". It got importance after the World Conference on Agrarian Reform and Rural Development, popularly known as WCARRD, held in Rome in 1979. It was stated that the "primary objective of rural development is the eradication of poverty, hunger and malnutrition. Essential contributory objectives include growth with equity, national self- reliance (especially in food production), ecological harmony and the conservation of natural resources. In pursuing these objectives, the participation of the intended beneficiaries including women is as important as the material results". As a result of WCARRD in 1979 many international,. governmental and non-governmental agencies have initiated process of participation of rural people particularly poor echelon of the society in the development process.

Institute of Development Studies (IDS), Sussex, and UK is a pioneer Institute in the world, which has been doing substantial works in the field of participation. According to IDS (1998), "Development organizations need to know how effective their efforts have been. But who should make these judgments and what basis"? With participatory approach, which involves local people, development agencies, and 12 and evaluation. Another technique for participatory development is "stake holder analysis." This is also a new one introduced from 1990s. World Bank, IMF and other international aid agencies widely use PRA/ stakeholder analysis for rural development projects. A few cases of 'beneficiary participation' from Eritrea, India and Pakistan are presented below.

In Eritrea importance of participation has been emphasized in the Constitution (1997). The article 8 and 22 of Eritrean constitution has clearly mentioned that, "the state shall work to bring about a balanced and sustainable development and shall use all available means to enable citizens to improve their livelihood in a sustainable manner, through participation......... in interest of present and future generations".

The first author visited different parts of Eritrea such as Maiduma of Debub region, Hagaz and Keren of Anseba region and Himbirty of Maakel region. It was observed that whether watershed or in cultivation of individual land, villagers enthusiastically participate. A few more examples can be cited here (Eritrea Profile, 26-8-2006). Local inhabitants and members of local defense force together implemented aforestation program at Adi-Keyih sub zone. With the participation of 3000 people more than 21000 meters of terraces have been developed and about 11000 eucalyptus seedlings have been planted. Another case is from Anseba region where students of Hagaz sub zone have dug more than 1200 meters long water pipelines. Students of Halhal sub zone carried weeding activities on farmland of 120 martyr families, besides; they repaired 2 kilometers of road. Thus, it is clear that ,villagers, defense forces, students and others participate in development works enthusiastically, which is really laudable. In India and Pakistan also the programs/projects meant for villagers assume participation of local inhabitants. Forestry program of India may be cited in this context, albeit many examples are there. For preservation of forest besides forest guard (government employees), local people have also been inducted by forming a committee popularly known as Vana Sanrakhsan Samity (VSS), i.e. Forest Preservation Committee.

VSS is formed every nook and corner of forestry projects of India. Like this in ma7477ny activities with participation of local inhabitants progress has been made in India.

There are many cases of participation in Pakistan also. Dir Area Support Program (DASP) is a case, which may be cited here. Dir is an area located in North West part of Pakistan. In this project with the participation of people supported by government officials various type of activities such as horticulture, growing of vegetables, crops etc. have been taken up. People enthusiastically participate in this type of activities. It has been working as a "Demonstration Effect" in other parts of Pakistan.

(*Source:* Horizon, EIT newsletter 20 December 2006)

# Index